Bush Lore

A Professional Hunter's Adventures in Central Africa

Adam Parkison

Published by Life Architect Media LLC

Copyright © 2025 by Adam Parkison

All Rights Reserved

ISBN: 979-8-218-61817-9

www.adamparkison.com

Table of Contents

Introduction.. vii

Chapter 1: The Bold Leopard............................... 1

Chapter 2: The Apprenticeship............................ 9

Chapter 3: Cutting Trails.................................... 17

Chapter 4: Buffalo Lessons................................. 25

Chapter 5: Nature's Classroom............................ 33

Chapter 6: The Bushbuck................................... 45

Chapter 7: The Rookie and the Giant Roan............ 51

Chapter 8: Picking a Fight................................... 57

Chapter 9: Lost... 69

Chapter 10: Cryptids of the African Bush............... 77

Chapter 11: Bozobo, Lord of the Savanna.............. 115

Chapter 12: Prince of Disaster............................. 121

Chapter 13: Careful Where You Step.................... 131

Chapter 14: Bongo, Lord of the Lowland Forest...... 137

Chapter 15: The Three Not-so-little Pigs................ 145

Chapter 16: A Safari of my Own.......................... 155

Chapter 17: The Hunters.................................... 163

Chapter 18: Stories in the Soil.............................175

Closing... 185

Acknowledgements.. 191

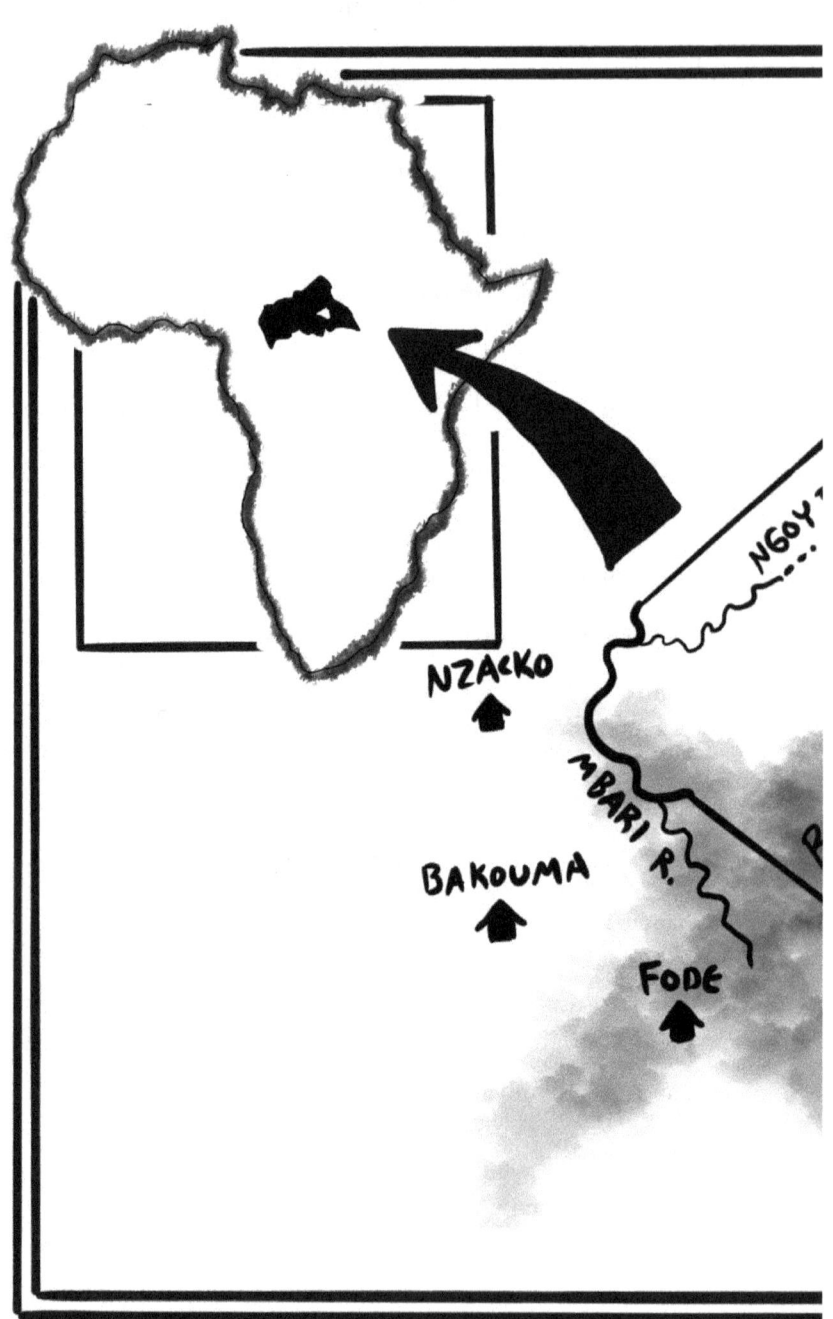

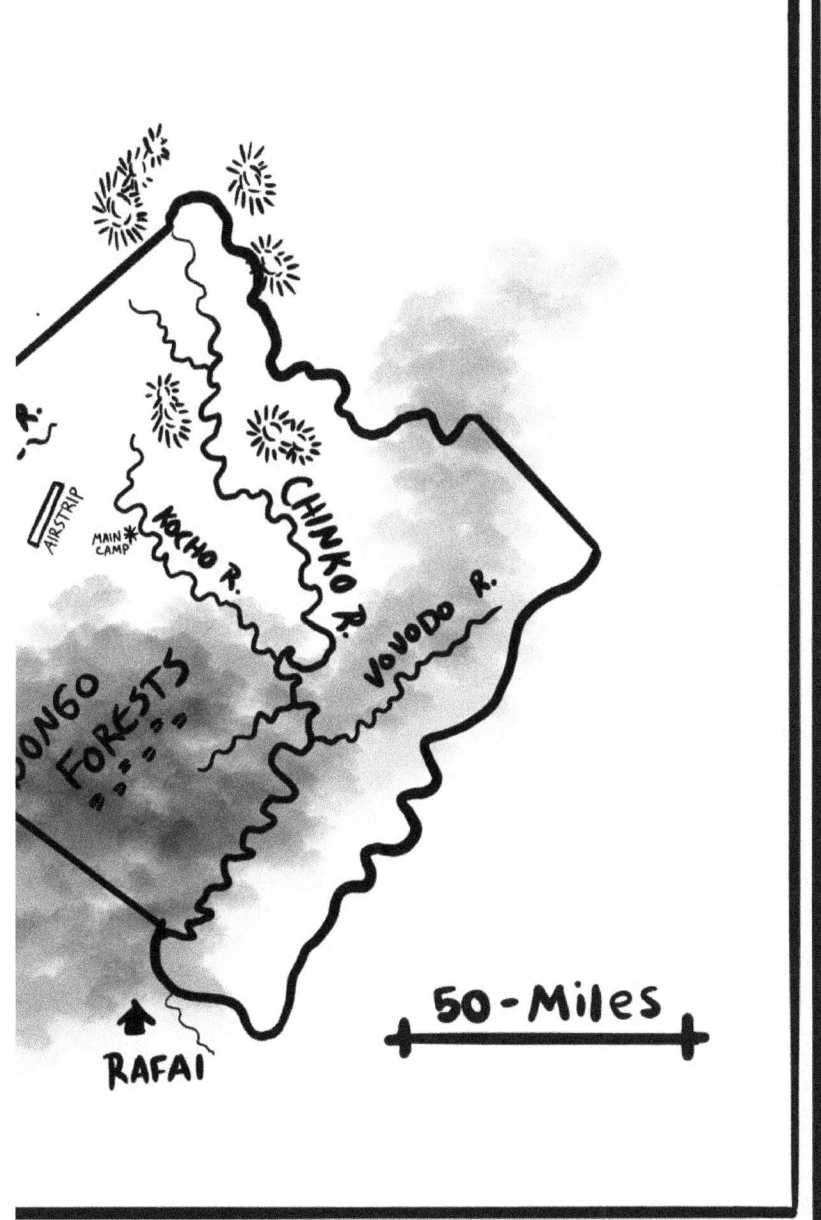

Introduction

When I first arrived in Central Africa in 2008 as a scrawny 19-year-old Kansan, the local African hunters wasted no time in giving me a nickname: *dengbe*. The meaning of the word in Sango, the local language, meant "blue duiker" - the smallest antelope found in those forests.

The name was meant to both mock me and to test my response to the insult. If there's one thing that fuels the Central Africans' sport of bullying, it's men who take themselves too seriously. But instead of taking the bait and reacting angrily to the nickname, I embraced it- much to the endearment of my African companions.

Besides, there was some truth to the title: I was the smallest, youngest, and most unassuming member of the company. In that foreboding African wilderness that greeted me upon my arrival, I knew I had to remain humble if I were to survive in that alien land. And so, I accepted this new title, "the blue duiker."

I was careful to hold onto this humility, even years later, after I had gained 30lbs of muscle and had earned a reputation as a successful Professional Hunter. So that even when my African friends began addressing me by my new title, *patron*, I had to remind them that I was still the *dengbe*.

The unexpected story of how I came to work in Africa as a Professional Hunter is almost unbelievable.

Nothing about my childhood would predict my future career on the game trails of the Dark Continent. I grew up in a completely non-hunting family. I was soft-spoken, non-confrontational, and had an overall gentle demeanor. As far as hunting was concerned, I was far more fascinated with wild creatures than I was the idea of killing them. But I did have an adventurous imagination that was fueled by the books I read; mostly, books about travel and exploration in exotic lands. I was far more interested in the characters of these stories than I was pop stars or sports athletes of the era; in turn, the heroes of my childhood made up the likes of Theodore Roosevelt, Lewis and Clark, David Livingstone, Henry Stanley, and more.

Africa became the object of my obsession when I first encountered the writings of Peter Hathaway Capstick. I distinctly remember reading *Death in the Long Grass* as a child, and immediately fantasized about my future life in the African bush as a Professional Hunter, chasing man-eating lions and marauding elephants.

Many of the books I read were stories of exploration from the turn of the twentieth century- at a time when adventure and hunting were synonymous with one another. I was not yet fully aware of the contemporary social shift toward sport hunting; or the nuances within the sport hunting community itself between the ethical sportsman and the more unscrupulous killers out there.

As someone who first admired animals before ever entertaining the idea of hunting them, I naturally held reverence for their lives. I only accepted the killing of certain individuals as a necessary step in completing the hunt, and not the reason for the hunt. I held to the motto hunter and philosopher Jose Ortega y Gasset famously wrote, "One does not hunt in order to kill. One kills in order to have hunted."

Growing up in a small Midwestern church community, many members of our congregation were diehard hunters; some even owned large tracts of hunting land and often showed off the photos of their successful hunts. But despite my eager interest in hunting and constant inquiries, not one of these men ever offered to take me hunting. Late in my teenage years, long after most hunters were well established in the field, my new neighbor at the time, Luis Prendes, went out of his way to mentor me in the outdoors. He might not ever know how much of an impact this decision had on my life during these formidable years. And now that I am an adult and father, I can fully appreciate the inconvenience it was for him to drag me along on his adventures.

Luis and I spent many days in the field together for three years, hunting Whitetail deer with archery equipment, catching Largemouth bass with light fishing tackle, and even spearfishing in the Florida Keys one summer. As it turned out, these experiences in the outdoors were the only experiences I had before impulsively leaving everything to pursue a career as a Professional Hunter in Africa.

In the summer of 2008, my life was perfectly planned and organized: I was a bank teller at a popular bank in town, I faithfully attended a community college, I was on track for a 4.0 GPA first semester, *and I was completely miserable*.

I continued to read my books about adventure, and my obsession with these stories bordered on madness. My only escape to the monotony of my dull life was in the pages of men who had lived a century before me. With every passing day spent in the boring Midwest, the life of adventure I longed for was slowly slipping away from me.

In desperation, I began sending unsolicited emails to various safari outfits across Africa. Most of these companies ignored me, but a few outright rejected me. Not only was I an American, but I had never left the United States before, and I had zero experience needed to work with dangerous animals in the African bush. No one wanted to hire me.

And then, I chanced upon a man who would change my fate forever: Erik Mararv.

I first read the name one day while following a rabbit hole on African safari forums online. In the *Hunting Report*, someone mentioned that the 23-year-old Swede had just started his own hunting outfit in the far eastern corner of a country called the Central African Republic, in a game reserve that had never been formally developed.

I did more research and discovered that Erik was a second-generation African-born Swede. His father had been drilling water wells across Central Africa for decades, and had earned a positive reputation among local governments; which in turn opened access to hunting land previously only reserved to local meat hunters. As a boy, Erik would travel with his father, and the two of them would set off on their own, hunting remote wilderness for buffalo, hippo, eland, and even elephant. At 18-years-old, Erik successfully passed his Professional Hunter's exam and began working for a French outfit in the game-rich northern reaches of the country; becoming the youngest PH at the time in Francophone Africa. After a few years, Erik decided to leave this company with the experience he had earned, and start his own outfit in the remote reaches of the Chinko basin. He called his company, CAWA safaris- short for "Central African Wildlife Adventures."

Joining Erik in his new hunting venture was his wife at the time, Emelie, also a Swede who grew up in a neighboring village near Cameroon, and their childhood friend, a Swede named Anton. Erik's own immediate family- his mother Gunnel, father Roland, and sister Charlotte- were also instrumental in the creation and operation of the outfit.

After reading about Erik, I decided to type up a hasty email, explaining my fascination with his work in the bush. I pressed send and did not expect how consequential that brief introduction would be. Imagine my shock when, a few weeks later, Erik responded. He patiently answered my inquiry about his work in the bush, and then- almost as an afterthought- offered me a job. I was completely stunned. The work, if I accepted, would start off as an unpaid internship, and my official title would be "Apprentice Professional Hunter." I would have to commit to nine months of work, but all my travel and living expenses would be paid for.

It is difficult to convey now, almost two decades later, the overwhelming doubt and anxiety I had about accepting the job and leaving the country for the very first time, to travel 7,000 miles away to work for strangers in the African bush. But after a lifetime of dreaming, the decision to go was immediate. Within a few short months, I would drop out of college, quit my job at the bank, and set off for the unknown.

The rest, as they say, is history.

This book is in no way written in chronological order, nor is it intended to be a narrative of my life in Africa. That role is already fulfilled by my forthcoming memoir, *East of Mbari* (working title). In many ways, writing that book was more difficult, because I had to take factual events and weave them in such a way as to paint a narrative arch, like a novel. This book, on the other hand, is a collection of my favorite stories that didn't make the cut for the memoir, but are no less exciting or meaningful to me. Some of these stories were previously published in various sportsmen magazines long ago and have only slightly been altered to fit the format of this book.

For a long time, I was disillusioned by my experiences with unethical hunters I met in the safari industry, and so I avoided writing about my work specifically as a PH, and instead, focused on the exploration and conservation work I did in Africa. But now, years later, as a proud hunter still pursuing game on public lands of the American West like my ancestors before me- I am drawn back to the subject of hunting; albeit carefully and with intention- the same way I approach the act of hunting itself. I recognize now that I am in a unique position to tell a story not many Americans have been blessed to tell. And so, for every young reader out there dreaming the same dreams that I had as a boy, it is my duty to share this story with you.

Chapter 1: The Bold Leopard

The orange sun was just dipping below the horizon as I sat next to my campfire. I was with a crew of local African employees, opening the old safari roads in preparation for the coming season. We were far in the bush, perhaps 30-miles away from the main safari lodge, and had just stopped at a makeshift campsite along a trickling stream for the night, and I had a lot on my mind. My first safari of the season was supposed to start soon with a two-week Lord Derby's eland hunt; but at the last moment, I got word that my would-be client had suffered a gunshot wound in a hunting accident in Europe and would no longer be joining me. In his place, a new hunter was coming, and this client had one animal on his mind: leopard.

Typically, a hunter in these parts needs three weeks set aside for pursuing leopard if they hope to be successful. My client had less than two weeks to hunt. So far that season, I had not come across the fresh sign of a mature leopard. The prospects of the approaching safari weighed heavy on my mind.

As I sat brooding on these thoughts, a troop of baboons downstream of our campsite suddenly went wild, hooting and screaming in alarm. Next, a flock of guinea fowl gawked a warning before fluttering away. The jungle folk were announcing the approach of a silent predator, and we didn't have to wait long to find out what it was. Just beyond the darkness of our campfires, a series of deep leopard grunts erupted like a motor engine, rising and falling with each breath.

Through the ages, writers have taken careful consideration in explaining the awe-inspiring sound of a lion's roar; but I'd argue, to hear a leopard's angry gurgles at close range can be just as intimidating.

"That leopard is no good," Charlemane, one of the African trackers said.

"You aren't afraid of leopard are you?" I asked, in feigned confidence.

"No," Charlemane said with a grin, "But no ordinary leopard comes up to a camp full of big men and chastises them like this. This cat here is a troublemaker."

All night that troublemaker let us know his disdain for our presence, keeping us wide awake with his angry grunts. This was all fine and well, until later in the night, when he came down among us.

In all my previous encounters with wild leopards, I have never once felt threatened by the animals. I have always been amazed by the behavior of the beautiful cats; curious, and yet clever. Bold, but mostly never malicious unless wounded. It was only when, at three o'clock in the morning, I stood at the edge of our camp urinating that I had to reassess my position on the subject of leopards.

As I stood there barefoot, with my pants pulled down in the most vulnerable position a man can find himself in, I began to notice a pair of glowing eyes illuminated by my headlamp at close range. As I quickly looked up, the leopard's face suddenly materialized in the beam of my light. I let out a weak cry before stumbling backwards with my pants around my ankles. The leopard- now satisfied he had made his point- let out a grunt from his flattened position no more than 20 yards distant before slipping away.

In the morning, after relaying my encounter to the other men, I discovered the same experience had happened to another of my workers.

In daylight, I walked alone along the forest edge, and found the fresh tracks of Red River hog, bushbuck, baboon and buffalo. Following a game path into the forest, a low grunting noise coming from a thick swampy area revealed the presence of a family of Red River hogs; too busy rooting in the mud to notice my presence. Continuing on, I found in a small section of soft soil, the fresh pug marks of the Tom leopard. They were large indeed, and I needed no convincing to tell me this animal was of trophy status. I spent the remaining morning finding a suitable bait tree and building a wall of grass panels in place of a future ground blind.

The notion of "baiting" sounds simple enough. The whole concept might even seem unfair to the uninformed observer: You simply hang a chunk of meat in a tree, and then sit in a blind and wait for a leopard to appear and simply take aim and fire- right? But hang a few baits in an area with a density of the big cats as high as they are in the southern Kocho river basin, and it doesn't take a person long to realize just how clever these spotted devils can be.

Not only must one hang the proper bait- since some leopards might not even approach a certain type of meat, while others might salivate over the same piece; but you must also put it in the right spot at the right time. Leopards walk the perimeter of their territory constantly, marking the boundary and checking to see if a competing cat or a prospective mate has encroached on their land. Since some Toms' territories are huge, it might take them a full week to return to a particular spot. A week-old bait in the hot African sun might be dry and useless by the time the leopard comes across it. Within such a huge territory, there are also "dead-zones" inside this area that the leopard simply has no reason to visit; hanging a bait here would be utterly pointless. So, one must learn by intuition, exactly the right spot to hang a bait. Otherwise, the hunters might find themselves with a dozen baits and not a single hit.

A couple weeks after the encounter with the big Tom, I returned to the spot with my trackers, and we hung a baboon carcass as bait in preparation for the safari that would soon begin in a couple days. We then hung five more baits in areas I knew were frequented by leopards.

As the clock trickled down, not one of the baits was hit by a cat. To add to my dismay, the morning of the hunt, my client never arrived. Shortly after, we received an email stating that the man had suffered a small heart attack and would no longer be coming. My hopes of the cat hunt were dashed.

But if there's one thing working in Africa teaches people, its to be flexible; when my boss Erik Mararv unexpectedly announced a week later that the same client would be coming the very next morning for the remaining five days of his booked safari, I wasted no time in checking the week-old bait sites. None of the other trees were touched. But arriving at the bait tree where we had been visited by the leopard the month before, I found claw marks on the trunk and a few nibbles on the baboon carcass. The sign was not very promising. None-the-less, I had my trackers quickly hang half a warthog carcass and hoped for the best.

Getting a leopard in only five days is simply unrealistic- but I also knew with hard work, and a bit of *bon chance*, anything was possible. With only one fresh bait hanging, I headed back to main camp to meet my client. The five-day clock had now officially started.

The one factor that did make the hunt quite interesting, was that my European hunter, George, spoke very little English. By very little- I mean, hardly any discernable words at all. This presented a challenge in itself. But the man was so good spirited and attentive, this lack of verbal communication did not hinder us much. Besides, he understood perfectly well simple words like, "shoot", or "don't shoot", and even, "big male." This small communication would be enough.

The second afternoon, after shooting and hanging more bait, we returned to the first bait site and found against all odds, the leopard had hit that very night. He had eaten much of one warthog leg, but there was still a fair bit of meat left. It was late in the afternoon, and instead of doing the right thing by backing off the site and coming back again the next day to avoid spooking the leopard, I hastily set up a blind. With only a couple hours of daylight, we got settled into the grassy shelter.

In the evening, we heard an animal slowly creeping out of the forest to our left. There was only the faint sound of sliding grass to signal the leopard's approach. The animal carefully walked around the blind before laying down parallel to us, apparently keeping watch of his prized meal in the tree. It was a tense few minutes while the cat was so close to us. I could hear the big Tom's chest rising and falling with each breath, and I feared he could hear my own heavy, shallow breathing.

Now I am no expert on leopard hunting, but after quite a few similar experiences, I lean toward the common belief of other hunters- including the famous cat hunter Jim Corbett- that leopards do not have the sharpest sense of smell. Either that, or they simply don't care much about unfamiliar smells. That afternoon the wind was blowing, and with the leopard so close and seemingly not paying attention to us, I believe if he did have a sharp nose he would have left long before then. Instead, he stood up and walked around the area suspiciously. He knew something was not right- and most probably our making the blind and disturbing the silence of the area earlier in the day had made him nervous.

For a long time, we heard nothing from the leopard. Just before dark, down the forest came the alarm chorus of a troop of baboons. Our leopard had left the area for the time being. Now it was dark, and there was no hope of taking the cat this day. Heading back to camp that night, I had a nervous knot in the pit of my stomach; I hoped my foolish decision to sit in the blind that night had not scared the cat for good.

The next day, we headed toward the blind bright and early. At one of the many creek crossings along the way, we spied a small crocodile suspended on the edge of a crystal-clear pool with rays of sunlight shining off its ancient body. The hunter implored me excitedly to catch it- an impulse I also shared. Soon, I was stalking the water's edge, as the hunter followed closely behind me, snickering like a happy child.

Just as I leaned over to grab the crocodile, I realized the creature was just a little too far out of reach. Giggling, the hunter grabbed me by my belt and motioned for me to lean forward. With him holding all my weight suspended over the water, I swiftly plucked the writhing reptile out, to the laughter of the entire team.

We snapped a few photos of the animal and then released it back into the water. As we left, the hunter was beaming. In broken English, he assured me, "We will get leopard now, the wilderness knows our heart pure. It will gift us with leopard!"

The night before, I had received a few tips from a couple of the top PHs working in camp, who suggested I pursue this leopard as if it were a big, clever house cat. This meant, the animal would be watching his bait closely for any intrusion. Rather than try and sneak into the blind and give the clever animal more reason to be suspicious, I decided to drive the truck right up to the blind. I also sent the trackers up into the tree to mess with the bait and make loud noises. I knew the Tom was big, and most probably would not take a liking to a couple of us hairless apes trying to steal his bait.

After the two of us got settled in the blind, the trackers started the engine and drove away talking loudly. After a few minutes, we heard an animal moving through the grass flanking us. It was clear the leopard had rushed out of his day bed to inspect his prized meal, just as my PH mentors had told me. However, the bait meat was covered in bees, and I felt certain the leopard would not actually climb the tree until the angry insects had left for the evening.

When hunting leopard, at times you can be fairly certain the animal is near, although never quite 100% positive. Even hearing the purring and light footsteps, I almost convinced myself it was all in my imagination as the hours dragged on. But just before dark, as the bees started to leave, there was a sharp sound of claws scraping on bark. Then the leopard was in the tree, filling a space that had been empty for hours. The sight of the large cat abruptly silhouetted against the sky made us both gasp.

I hissed, a little too zealously in exaggerated English, "Big male! Shoot!"

I held my breath, and then the deathly quiet was disturbed by the booming shot. The leopard took a weak leap and tumbled down the tree. There was rustling in the leaves and a futile roar- before all went quiet.

The cat died not far from where it had fallen. We were overwhelmed at the sight of the large Tom sprawled out on the ground. Brushing my hand over its fur, I thought about the night a month before when the same cat had visited me. The beast very well could have known we were there in the blind, but his boldness became his undoing. George stayed quietly next to the animal, caressing its fur in complete reverence.

When my trackers arrived after the shot, it was by now dark and they could not see the cat. They asked me eagerly if we had been successful. With as much feigned disappointment as I could muster, I stared at the ground, and then said under my breath, "Tonight, a big leopard is… dead."

The trackers went wild when they heard this. They lifted George off the ground and began dancing and shouting.

When we arrived in main camp two hours later, the party there was only just beginning. The entire camp staff met us around the guest houses, and the celebration continued for over an hour. Charlemane and the other locals who had been with me opening roads a month before came to inspect the beast that had terrified them that dark night.

"I told you that leopard was no good," he said smiling, patting me on the back in congratulations.

In the rush of excitement, George the client turned to me with a face full of smiles, "I'm very happy!" he said in broken English. "I have tried on two previous safaris for leopard, and this," he said pointing at the cat, "This, is my very first leopard!"

I smiled shyly as he turned away to join the dancing crowd once again. I kept my mouth shut; I didn't want to ruin the evening by telling George, this was also *my* first leopard hunt.

Chapter 2: The Apprenticeship

Of all the hunts I partook in during my time in Africa, one hunt stands out in my memory as the greatest. Ironically, I did not guide this particular hunt. I was an apprentice, tagging along while my boss Erik Mararv guided. This safari had everything- from baiting leopards, tracking Giant eland, getting lost alone in the bush, and finally- shooting a big buffalo bull with a double-barreled express rifle.

Although the bulk of my apprenticeship took place out in the bush with the local Africans learning firsthand how to track, decipher animal sign, and general bush craft skills- the finer details of interacting with the clients was learned by shadowing a Professional Hunter on safari. And Erik Mararv was a master to learn from. Having grown up in the bush and hunting with his father since the time he could walk, hunting with him was like hunting with the indigenous Africans.

The client on this particular safari was an energetic Austrian man who was probably in his late forties but had the vitality of a man half his age. He would prove to be one of the most ethical, hardworking hunters I would ever meet.

The Austrian's safari would take place in the north-central region of our hunting concession called Ngoy, named after a clear spring creek that ran through the area. Ngoy differed in many ways to the typical rainforest mosaics found in the Chinko basin in that it was almost exclusively savanna woodland checkered with groves of acacia trees and the odd palm trees. I have not yet seen the Selous Game Reserve in Tanzania, but from the photos, Ngoy seems to share some parallels.

The target species was Lord Derby's eland, and we took every opportunity to pursue the animals whenever we came upon fresh tracks. It was on these stalks that I would learn eland hunting was a numbers game: how many hours would be spent on the trail before luck shined on us. On most days, the long pursuit would end in the animals winding us and fleeing into oblivion. If we followed the tracks enough, in time, we would get lucky and the animals would make a mistake. I also learned, unlike other animals, the only surefire way of getting a shot at a Giant eland was to make an educated guess on the herd's movement and then try to intercept them. I distinctly remember the first time I saw Erik use this strategy, and how we very nearly secured a big bull early in the hunt.

We had been following the eland from daybreak until late in the afternoon, only managing to get brief glimpses of the animals through the thick brush. The tracking team carried food, water, and rifles for Erik and the client- but I was left to my own devices. Ignorantly, I only carried a single water bottle for myself, which I had been nursing in small sips to try and conserve. I was also given the client's impossibly heavy .470 Nitro Express double rifle to carry, "In case we ran into buffalo." It was in this state we followed the animals, while the heat bore down on us, and the hordes of mopani flies overwhelmed us.

I was praying for Erik to give up and call it a day when we finally spotted the ghostly tan animals skirt around a very small patch of forest, headed for a funnel in the hills on the opposite end. This was the chance Erik had been waiting for. Frantically, the hunting team with Erik in the lead began sprinting to get ahead of the moving animals, intending to intercept them at the funnel on the far end of the forest.

When we reached the spot, I was panting like a dog and severely dehydrated. I watched as Erik and the Austrian lay down behind some bushes 100 yards in the distance as the first animals began to move past them. An old bull stood in the middle of the milling animals, tantalizingly out of reach as cows and calves blocked the shooting lane.

As I lay behind my own bush trying to look small, I heard snapping of branches from the patch of forest, and soon watched a handful of cow eland emerge feeding steadily toward me. I looked to Erik frantically, hoping to hear the report of the client's rifle- but it never came. Then, one of the cow eland came within 5 yards from where I lay crouched, and began feeding on some bushes.

By now, the animal loomed impossibly big over me, and I became frightened by her sheer size. As if to reiterate this imposing position, she bent her head down so her horns became intertwined with the bush, and with one clean swipe, effortlessly tore it from the ground. Eventually, some of the animals began to spook- presumably from winding us- and within a few minutes, the animals were storming away in a cloud of dust. After re-grouping, Erik decided to give chase again. We would follow them until dark if we had to.

This time I was nervous about getting so close to the animals again, and so I quietly stayed back even farther and observed the hunt at a distance. I always made sure to keep Erik and the trackers within eyesight in the savanna woodland, but in one brief moment of distraction, I lost sight of them. The landscape wasn't too dense, and so I expected to catch up to them again. But when I got to the spot where I last saw them- I found only empty bush. I followed what I thought were the fresh eland tracks for about a mile or so, but when they arrived at one of our 4x4 roads, I realized the tracks were old.

Deciding it was better to stay on an established road than risk getting lost even further, I started heading toward the direction I thought camp lay. Since this was my first time in the area and I had no sense of the roads, my chosen direction was merely a blind guess. Unfortunately, I would choose the farthest road network to camp - and ironically, the only road Erik did not send the search party who were out looking for me.

For the remaining 3 hours of daylight, I walked that lonely, dusty road, carrying only my empty water bottle and the client's heavy double rifle. The bush was bone dry and eerily silent. At one point the road began flanking a dense, 1-mile-long thicket, and my primal senses were on high alert at this shady area. As if on cue, I stumbled on a pile of fresh lion tracks and scat full of waterbuck hair. My anxiety shot up instantly and I began to look around me obsessively. Within a few minutes of leaving the lion scat, I spooked a Warthog boar who tore through the bush a few yards off the road, nearly killing me from fright. It was in this moment that I decided to break open the rifle breach and make sure I had bullets in the event of an emergency: to my horror, the rifle was empty. If I were to be attacked by a wild animal in that moment, I would only be able to use the rifle as a heavy club.

Late in the evening, I arrived to a network of small hippo ponds supplied by a tiny trickle of spring water bubbling out of the hills in the distance. It was the first water I had come across, and by now I had been nearly 4 hours without a drink. Despite the animal droppings and thin layer of slime floating on top, I got on my knees and began eagerly lapping up the liquid. I knew this was going to give me intestinal problems, but I was too desperate to care. With fresh hippo tracks in the mud around me, I hurried on, knowing the animals would emerge from their dark lair around sunset to feed on the fresh grass flanking the ponds. I also knew the camp was only a mile or so away.

As I finally approached camp, my face was burning with embarrassment. I could barely look Erik in the eyes as I approached him standing in the staff quarters, trying my best to look carefree from the ordeal. Thankfully, the only expression Erik gave was one of relief at having turned up safely. The client was also a little more than relieved to see his beloved double rifle returned to him.

Throughout the safari I was responsible for collecting leopard baits- usually baboon or warthog- and then hanging and checking them at suitable bait trees. Tricking a mature Tom leopard into taking the bait was a difficult skill in itself, as was finding a location in which a cat would cross. Inevitably, this gave me a lot of hands-on experience in the art, which I would later use on my own leopard hunts. Incidentally, my preoccupation in these tasks also meant I missed some of the action taking place on the safari. I missed the day the Austrian got his eland. I also missed the evening he got his leopard. Still, I was having a blast on the hunt, and the remaining days were no less eventful.

Before the safari concluded, we ended up having ourselves "a grand buffalo hunt" – as the Austrian called it.

With a fresh carpet of green grass covering the rolling hills of Ngoy, we picked up the trail of a herd of buffalo crossing the road at first light. In less than an hour, we glimpsed the animals feeding in the distance. The wind was aimed perfectly in our faces, and the hills offered enough contour to easily sneak up to the animals. Up to that point, everything was working in our favor, and I suspiciously waited for our luck to change.

Erik and the Austrian sat crouched behind a fallen tree, with the herd of buffalo feeding across an open hillside immediately in front of us. I hid behind some bushes alongside the trackers, 50 yards distant. The big herd bull strutted with stiff legs through his milling herd of cows and calves. As he moved, it became clear his intended path would lead him directly in front of the hunters' ambush. The bull closed the distance from 150 yards down to a mere 50 yards, and I watched the hunter slowly exchange his scoped rifle for the iron sighted .470 Nitro Express double rifle. Even today, over a decade later, I can clearly see the image of that memory in front of me.

With an angry bellow and violent head-butt, the bull directed one of his lingering cows back into the herd, then he stood alone, broadside to the hunters. The fibers of his limbs twitched tensely, and every feature of his muscles rippled in the morning light. He was magnificent. And in an instant, the picture changed completely as one barrel barked from the double rifle. In the morning dew I could see a vapor trail shoot out from the end of the rifle and into the animal's shoulder. The bull stumbled headlong down the hill, trying his utmost to remain upright as he staggered under the weight of his failing body, his eyes wild with fear and rage. Then the second barrel barked, and the bull crumbled face down in the dirt, legs lifting in the air in a near summersault.

Even before the last of the herd had thundered away in the distance, and before we could reach the place where the bull lay in a heap, we knew it was over from the forlorn death bellow released from the bull's final breath. Then it was all over, and the real work of the hunt began.

No matter how many hunts I undertake, or how many animals I kill, the one aspect of hunting that I have been unable to get used to is the immediate aftermath proceeding a successful hunt. There is an uncomfortable, obtrusive feeling that washes over me the moment I take my sharp knife out and begin cutting into the meat of the slain animal. As the blade slices through muscles and tendons, turning an intricate creature into manageable chunks of flesh- I feel a sense of regret for what I have done. This emotion does not automatically equate to moral guilt, as some anti-hunters might suggest, but rather, humility. It is a reminder of our shared mortality, and the fragile biological make-up of our flesh.

This feeling I am describing- from the true hunter- cannot be felt simply by pulling the trigger and ending an animal's life; it must also be felt in that final step, turning the animal into useable parts by the crudest means available. Many, but not all, of the wealthy elite who go on African hunting safaris have never experienced this feeling. And in some ways, I cannot respect them as hunters, no matter how many trophies line their walls. The Austrian was a true hunter in every sense of the word.

When we walked up to the fallen bull, the man got on his knees, took his hat off his head, and bowed with eyes closed in respect. Then, he ripped some blades of grass from the ground and stuffed them in the mouth of the buffalo- as was hunting tradition in old European ceremony. After this, he pulled a small flask of alcohol out of his shirt pocket, took a shot for himself, and then poured a small shot out on the ground for the buffalo.

When he had finished, the Austrian began immediately cutting the buffalo up with the help of the African trackers. Soon, the man was sweaty and covered in gore. One tracker made a small fire to ward off some aggressive bees which had arrived interested in the mineral-rich blood on the ground. When the bull was completely quartered and the animal's parts lay scattered on top of leafy piles on the dirt, the purple liver was soon located and thrown on the fire. It was the Africans' tradition to immediately cook and devour the liver after a successful buffalo hunt.

As the organ was lifted off the fire, still leaking purple froth, the Africans began to cut it up into chunks and eat it. They shared some pieces with Erik and I, but they did not offer any to the Austrian. Up to that point, no client had ever shown an interest in eating the gruesome cuisine. But the Austrian was different. He suddenly jumped in, demanding to partake in the feast with everyone else. Greedily grabbing a piece of liver, his teeth tore through the purple, frothing organ. The Africans loved the gesture and cheerfully slapped him on the back, calling him a true hunter.

On one of the last evenings on safari with the Austrian- I was walking down a footpath in camp toward the dining area, accompanied by Erik and his wife Emelie, headed to join the client for dinner. We were talking about the man and remarking on how comfortable he seemed in the African bush, despite his "white collar" life in Europe. He wasn't just a tourist to babysit, we all agreed, but one of the team members who held his own. As we rounded a bend and the full Kocho river came into view, Erik and Emelie both let out a gasp.

The Austrian man was naked, paddling in a backstroke in the middle of the Kocho river without a care in the world. His pale white skin almost glowed in contrast to the black water, and he was repeatedly sucking water in his mouth and then shooting it out in a fountain, like a child does in a bathtub.

"Sir, there are crocodiles in there!" Emelie shouted, and I followed up with my own warnings, having just seen a monster of the species just downstream not long before.

The man shooed us away with the flick of his wrists, smiling devilishly and continuing on with his swim, even as the night approached.

"He is indeed comfortable in the bush," Erik said wryly, "Maybe too comfortable."

Chapter 3: Cutting Trails

One of the less glorified roles of the apprentice Professional Hunter, is the task of "road cutting." This entails going out with a group of local Africans deep in the bush, following designated GPS way points, and carving out new tracts of 4x4 roads with axes, shovels and machetes. Although many PHs consider this to be an inferior job reserved for the lowest men in the company- to me, this was where the real adventure took place.

Imagine given nearly complete freedom to explore previously untrodden bush for weeks at a time, hunting game birds and antelope for meat, and then fishing crystal clear forest streams with a flashlight at night. This was the time I was mentored in the art of tracking and animal sign by my African companions. These guys were masters of the wilderness, and the more eager I was to learn from them, the more enthusiastically they taught me.

They patiently show me edible and medicinal plants, and other bushcraft skills. I ate good during these times, supplementing my bland ration of *gozo* (manioc root powder cooked into a dough) with forest duiker meat, wild yams, wild salad greens and even feral peppers. We sometimes found wild Congo coffee plants growing in the dry plateaus, whose cherries we ate raw or baked for a lightly roasted wild coffee drink.

We had many unexpected visitors at our remote campsites in the bush. My first elephant encounter occurred during a road cutting expedition, when two of the giant beasts came blundering through our campsite late on a moonless night. Another night, along the Chinko river, a large bull hippopotamus approached our sleeping forms along the banks and began bellowing loudly, spinning in circles in the shallows, splashing and honking in anger. Still another time, a leopard killed a baboon in the trees above us, and then devoured its meal not far from where we lay next to our extinguished campfires. Nearly every night on our road expeditions, the air was filled with the roars of lions, the yipping of hyenas, and more unsettling- the screams of the mysterious tree hyraxes.

During the day, I would often take off on our lunch breaks and explore the new areas on foot. I remember stumbling on a large, solitary buffalo in the long grass, and silently following his polished horns as he moved at a leisurely pace. On a rare occasion, I even came upon a massive herd of eland feeding along a hillside in a picturesque setting of bright green grass and a baby blue skyline in the background.

Away from the bustling sounds of the busy main camp, one could never guess what they might see out there in the bush. Once, we even spooked a pair of bongo antelope traversing the grassland. The sight of their mythical red and white striped fur in that unexpected landscape was surreal. Similarly shocking, was the time I stumbled upon a large male lion sleeping in the long grass. The cat was as equally surprised as I was, and thankfully made no fuss about our meeting.

The African men who joined me on these trips were obsessed with only one thing: fishing.

When I say "fishing," I don't mean with standard hook and line- although we did occasionally employ this method. Typically, the men would fish by wading in the clear, shallow streams at night, armed with their machetes. The large catfish that occupied these streams would hunt at night, emerging from their burrows under logs and steep banks where they rested during the day. The size of some of these fish were startling in the context of the tiny streams in which they occupied. Walking quietly through the water, the bright light from the men would momentarily blind the fish, giving the men time to carefully dispatch them with a swift strike from their machetes. Occasionally, we came upon small and medium sized crocodiles in these streams, but we left these animals unmolested.

One fish we avoided was the electric catfish. This particular species manufactures genuine electrical currents deep within its organs and then distributes it through its thick outer skin. This species has been described by historians for hundreds of years, and was even used in ancient Egypt to treat certain neurological ailments. A shock from these fish was always uncomfortable- but a strike from one of the larger specimens could be dangerous.

Once, while wading through a dark, deeper jungle stream, my leg brushed up against the side of a large electric catfish and the shock momentarily paralyzed my entire leg. I screamed, thinking I was being pulled under by a crocodile, and my loyal African mates had to drag me out, laughing hysterically when they realized what had happened. Just like all the other bushcraft, I became nearly equally as good at machete fishing as my African counterparts.

The only other activity the Africans loved on these road cutting expeditions, was raiding bee hives for fresh honey. This was as hazardous and painful as one can imagine- and just like the other activities, I felt equally obliged to participate in.

The process for raiding a beehive was pretty standard each time. Once a large hive was located inside a hollow tree trunk, plans were made for an attack. Raiding the hive almost always occurred at night out of necessity to avoid getting attacked by the angry bees, since the insects couldn't see in the dark. Sometimes, we had to build small ladders to get to the hive if it was located high in a tree. A specific type of herbal leaf grew in the bush that- when lit on fire- created a smoke that dazed the bees. After the entrance to the hive was excavated enough to allow for a man's arm to fit into, flaming grass torches were used with the herbal bundle to smoke out the angry bees.

Each man would intermittently smoke the hive out, and then thrust his arm into the hollow tree trunk to pull out the large honeycombs. Although the smoke would prevent the bees from outright attacking our faces, it still didn't prevent the bees from stinging us randomly as we reached into the hive. It was not uncommon for a person to receive dozens of stings in a matter of minutes. During my time in Africa, I raided four different bee hives with my African friends; something that earned me a legendary reputation among the men, since no other Westerner in our entire company (or any other *munju* they had ever encountered) ventured to try it. This, more than anything else, endeared me to the men.

I enjoyed this road cutting work so much, even when I became an accomplished licensed Professional Hunter and no longer had an obligation to do such tasks, I would still voluntarily lead expeditions into new country during my free time. I could not get enough of the raw adventure these trips brought me.

Just like all work in the bush, road cutting expeditions were not without their hazards.

For starts, the sheltered forests where we camped held colonies of angry Safari ants. These creatures would typically remain underground for most of the day and only make their appearance in the middle of the night when it was most inconvenient to address them. We would awake to a carpet of thousands of angry red ants covering our entire campsite- sometimes caking the blankets we were wrapped in, biting us in the hundreds and latching onto our skin with their vice-like mandibles. An animal carcass, left unattended on the forest floor, would be completely picked clean of all flesh in a single night by the ants. In the event of an ant attack late at night, we would boost up our campfires and then take the hot coals and scatter them around us to form a barrier to keep the ants at bay.

I have previously written about the various injuries myself and my men suffered, most notably- a man who suffered a compound fracture of his arm (which I described in my other book). On another expedition, a man was in the process of swinging down an axe, when the heavy iron head came off, cracking him on the skull with the sharp edge, knocking him unconscious and requiring a dozen stitches to treat. Another time, I cared for a man who had swung a machete down on a tree trunk but missed, and drove the blade between his big toe and the next toe, splitting it far into his foot where the long tendons attached to the bones.

Besides injuries, we also suffered from various illnesses and parasitic infections. On one trip, a man had been complaining about eye pain for days, but every time I checked his eye, I could see nothing. Finally, fearing he might be suffering from a filaria worm, I instructed the man to close his eye for a long moment. Then, with a bright flashlight aimed at the spot, I told him to open his eyes quickly: sure enough, a small, almost translucent worm could be seen swimming across his cornea.

On this very same expedition, some of the men had to help evacuate me to main camp after I was hit with amoebic dysentery suddenly. The illness hit me so fast, I went from hiking strong one morning, to being carried back to our camp by two men a few hours later. During the night, I defecated more than a dozen times, until only blood exited my body, and I was too weak to even stand. Luckily, our main camp had enough antibiotics in supply to treat me, and within a couple days I was back to normal.

One hazard that was often overlooked during these road cutting expeditions, were bush fires. In the dry season lasting from November to March, the grass blanketing the thick bush becomes bone dry and brittle. This process happens almost overnight, as plains of lush, head high grass transform into yellow straw. Under such conditions, even the smallest spark could turn into a raging fire sweeping across the hills, fanned by relentless summer winds. It seems obvious then that this would be a danger; however, we grew careless of this threat because we were often the ones setting the fires in order to clear the brush for new growth.

We minimized the threat of the fires by joking about them. One night around the campfire, a client asked Erik, "What is the protocol if a vehicle gets stuck and a bushfire threatens to consume it?"

Erik laughed, "Well, my first advice for whoever was driving the vehicle, would be to run straight to South Sudan or suffer my wrath for destroying my car!"

Everyone laughed, but then Erik became more somber.

"In all seriousness, if a vehicle gets stuck in a tough spot during a bush fire- whether its from mechanical failure or some other reason- the best thing to do is to take out machetes and shovels and try to get a fire break around the vehicle. Then- and this the most important part- they would need to set the grass on fire close to them. That way, the flames can start small and burn outward, away from the vehicle as they grow."

I remember this conversation distinctly, because a few years later, Erik's instructions would replay in my head verbatim when I found myself in this very situation.

The disaster happened clumsily and with very little time to react. We were driving through the long grass of a well-established route, throwing matches into the grass behind us setting it ablaze as we puttered on harmlessly out of the reach of the flames. It was an exercise we had done a hundred times before without incident. But this time, all of a sudden, our vehicle drove on top of an unseen tree branch resting across the road and stopped with a jarring crunch. Although the branch was relatively thin and weak, it had gotten so tangled around the drive-axle, we were utterly helpless to move.

We were calm at first since the grass fire was still some distance off, burning in the opposite direction. But in an instant, the wind turned, and the wall of flames came barreling down on us. I turned to look at the other men, and their eyes revealed what I also felt: shear panic.

I grabbed the shovels and machetes off the back of the truck and screamed directions at my lead tracker, Charles, who immediately understood what I meant to do. The four of us began to cut the brush around the truck and then, with shovels, dug a shallow fire break around us like a mote. Once we had a crude barrier etched in the dirt, we began working to grow the fire break around the truck. As the flames grew closer around us, I knew it was now or never. Although I wanted the fire break to be larger- we were out of time. Reluctantly, I told the men to start lighting the grass around us.

At first, the two other less experienced men looked at me in horror, but Charles reassured them that this was the right decision. Hesitantly, they lit the grass, and the flames grew around us. The heat climbed noticeably, and the ash from the newly lit grass began to stick to our bodies that were now covered in sweat. As the larger flames rolled toward us from the wind-born fire, the smaller flames from the fire break met them at just a distance to avoid consuming the vehicle. For a moment, it seemed like all the oxygen in our small bubble was snuffed out, and I choked and coughed, praying for the black cloud of smoke around us to clear.

And just like the wave of a breaking tide, the fire passed over and around us. The sky once again shown bright blue, and predatory birds like black kites soured above us, snatching up the flying insects that swarmed in retreat away from the flames. The fire continued to roll across the landscape, clearing the horizon as far as the eyes could see. Our truck stood there in the only small patch of un-burnt soil.

The men and I lay on the ground, panting like exhausted dogs. I looked into the eyes of Charles, and noted that I had never seen him so stressed before. But in an instant, his serious demeanor suddenly exploded in laughter, and we all began laughing. In the Africans' world, near-disastrous experiences were apart of daily life and not something to dwell on. We continued on with our work, barely remarking on the close call we had just had.

That very same year, miles away in a different area of the hunting block, an all-African crew of road cutters found themselves in a similar situation when their vehicle became stuck, high-centered on a large termite mound. But these unfortunate men did not have time to make a fire break around their truck- and as the flames came barreling down on them, they abandoned the vehicle and fled on foot across the waterless landscape. The rust on the old Toyota Hilux was so deep, once the flames caught, it nearly incinerated the entire vehicle. The only evidence that a truck had been there was a molten drive-train laying in the red dirt.

Alas, despite all these dangers, much of our time spent in the bush was full of adventure and excitement- albeit, always sprinkled with hard work. There was something pleasing to the senses to be able to look backwards at the end of a long day and physically see the results of our efforts stretched out in the miles of new 4x4 track. In this way, our hard work was rewarded with tangible results we could see and touch.

Even now, as I jot down these stories from my home in the mountains of Colorado- it is not the dangerous or grandiose hunting safaris I think about most when I think about Africa. It is the less remarkable memories from the road cutting expeditions that stand out to me. It is the melancholy orange sun descending behind mopani trees, setting the world ablaze in its departure; it is the soundtrack of the bellowing lion and coughing leopard against the immense black canvas of stars; it is waking up in the cold morning, squatting around a fire, sipping on coffee with my family of dark faces. And it is my dream that someday, in the future, I can return there.

Chapter 4: Buffalo Lessons

Walking up to the buffalo, I felt nothing but elation at seeing his wide horns and unmoving body. No other thought entered my mind, apart from the fact that my client's buffalo was dead. Lung blood dripped from his mouth, and his eyes were glazed over and dormant. I was congratulating my hunter when a quiet voice spoke up behind me. It was George, a Central African PH. He suggested I load my .458 Lott rifle. I looked at him, and then back at the motionless buffalo, confused.

"They don't die *that* easily," George said.

I followed his instructions, and from the time I chambered the cartridge and had taken ten more steps, the buffalo- to my horror- was suddenly upright, staggering to its feet with furry in its eyes, trying to regain his balance before the charge.

I heard George's calm voice in the background, repeating in his French accent, *"Attention! Attention!"*

My hunter and I continued taking turns firing into the animal, as its blocky head pressed forward, staggering with each shot. Finally, after sending my last .458 Lott into the animal's spine above its lowered boss, the animal fell for good. Even as it lay there expelling its loud, haunting death bellow, its eyes still shown with rage.

After the incident, I couldn't stop thinking about what would have happened if George had not spoken up and snapped me into concentration, when I thought the hunt was over. It is easy to criticize someone else's actions from an outside perspective, but during the heat of the moment, even foolish mistakes can be made.

During my apprenticeship, and then the preceding years as a licensed PH, I have made my share of mistakes. But mistakes are only wasted if one does not learn from them and warn others from repeating the same errors. For me, learning the ropes as a guide in Central Africa came primarily through the endless buffalo safaris I started my hunting career with; here is where small, yet dangerous errors were made, and also the exhilarating triumphs that came from a well-executed hunt.

I began guiding a handful of safaris under the careful watch of George my second year in the Central African Republic. It was a blessing for me to be mentored by a local hunter, because unlike the other "white" PHs who had good, self-learned hunting skills and strategies- George had the extra advantage of the more subtle skills like sharp eyesight, hearing, and a primal sixth sense that came easy to a man born and raised in the bush. I looked and listened eagerly to absorb as much bushcraft from him as I could.

George was a particularly good PH to learn the art buffalo hunting from because he had an intimate respect for the animal that few of us could share; just under his solar plexus, he wears a deep, ghastly scar caused by one of the creatures. During his early years of poaching, he learned the hard way what it felt like to make a mistake when following up on a wounded buffalo.

He was hunting with a homemade shotgun and had followed the buff into a thicket after shooting it once. He barely made it two steps into the bush before the animal was on top of him. The bull apparently thought punching a hole in George's torso was enough to finish the job, and blessedly left after flooring the man. George eventually recovered and went on to become an expert tracker and anti-poacher after the incident.

The Central African Savanna buffalo looks like the offspring of a Cape buffalo and Dwarf forest buffalo union. Within a herd-numbering no more than 30 in the eastern Central African Republic- you might find an even variety of both red and black animals. The shape of the horns also vary, sometimes wide, curved, and flat on top like Cape buffalo; and other times short, and back-sweeping like Dwarf forest buffalo. The variety in these physical features make the animal unique, though it might be smaller and less glorified than its Cape buff cousin. It is of the opinion of many experienced African hunters that the Savanna buffalo is far less temperamental, and often downright gentle compared to the "black death" buffalo of eastern and southern Africa. But this opinion might not be accurate.

Firstly, the areas that central and west African Savanna buffalo inhabit, are far less populated by humans. And large human pressure equals a large number of poachers. With hunters walking around the bush with homemade weapons, the number of wounded- and ultimately pissed off- buffalo suddenly rises. In other words, the Savanna buffalo are usually more naive than Cape buffalo, and haven't yet learned their enemy as intimately in the remote areas they live in. Just ask my friend and mentor, PH Christophe Morio, and he will tell you the temperament of the Savanna buffalo; he wears the scar across his throat, from a wounded Savanna buff that nearly tore out his esophagus. And my other French PH mentor, Phillipe Clero, who says in all the charges from buffalo he has experienced in twenty years of guiding throughout both the CAR and Tanzania, the Savanna buffalo for him has proven to be the most hell-bent on revenge; and in fact, is the only animal to ever touch him and a client. Though by dumb luck, no one was seriously hurt in the charge.

Taking all things into consideration and learning from my mistake that early safari, I decided to be sharper from then on when pursuing buff. One of my next safaris, I had a chance to make good with a follow-up during a bad situation.

It was just before dark, and my client made a snapshot on a big, black bull. I couldn't tell much from the reaction of the animal after being shot, but something just didn't feel right. George also felt my same hesitation. For about 200 yards we followed the bloody spoor, until the trail started winding in and out of thick cover.

Taking this as a sign to back off and reassess the situation, we broke off to the left which offered a rocky outcrop to better view the area into which the animal's tracks disappeared. Not long after arriving at the spot, we caught sight of a black form, laying just ahead of where we had left the trail. In typical sinister buffalo fashion, the animal had circled his back trail in a J-hook and was waiting to ambush us. Luckily, we were now watching him from the side, and he was oblivious to our new location.

The hunter fired off a shot, but the buffalo barely flinched. He shot again and again- but the animal remained motionless. Frustrated, I began shooting as well. After my second perfectly placed shot, I knew something strange was going on. Carefully creeping up closer to the buffalo- which was still standing upright and staring straight ahead- we discovered the animal had fallen with its head and horns between the crook of a small tree. The animal was dead by the time we arrived to its bizarre position.

A potential ambush averted: this was a triumph for my early days as a buffalo hunter, and I was grateful we took the time to carefully assess the situation rather than blunder behind the trail of the wounded animal.

A person won't become an expert buffalo hunter overnight, and despite another full year of guiding buffalo safaris without an incident, there were still mistakes and lessons to be learned. One of these errors occurred the next season, and though it luckily didn't result in an incident- I still knew I had made a grave mistake that almost cost us our lives.

It all started when my friend made a shot on a buffalo at about 120 yards in a wide, open meadow. Though a bit far to shoot at a buffalo, my friend had proven himself to be a good shot previously, and I had no reason to doubt his taking a shot then. But somewhere in the sweaty hands and jerky eyes, I should have picked up on his nervousness. In the heat of the moment, he made a bad shot. How bad exactly, no one could say for sure. The incident occurred just before dark, and all that was left of the buffalo's presence was a cloud of dust.

"Let's just walk up ahead a little to check things out," I suggested.

Cautiously, we moved between fresh green grass along the edge of a forest. When we arrived to a spot of dense scrub, I instructed the hunter to remain with one tracker while I and two others scouted ahead. I knew by then from the poor blood trail that the shot was very bad indeed. But it seemed the injured buffalo had kept up with the herd and was continuing on as usual. My hope was to catch the herd before dark, and maybe get another shot into the injured buffalo. I assumed from the animal's reaction at being hit, and from the thin blood, that it was perhaps a flesh wound. But of course, there was no way for me to know for sure, and it was lazy eagerness that pushed me forward. What I didn't know, was that the buffalo was not keeping up with the herd, and its injury was far more serious.

Unable to catch the fleeing animals, and with the sun nearly gone, we returned to where we left our hunter. By the time we met their headlamps on the road, visibility was down to nothing. We had returned the way we came, walking past a dense wall of scrub. We passed this spot and were headed back to the truck, when we suddenly heard rustling in the foliage where we had just been standing. By now, it was pitch dark, and we could see absolutely nothing beyond a few yards.

Suddenly, a very large animal began moving with difficulty from the thicket. In painful grunts, the wounded buffalo bellowed its rage as it began moving away from us.

As we listened, I felt my stomach turning and thought I would vomit. I had been incredibly stupid to leave my hunter in such a precarious spot and blunder forward so carelessly myself. For the rest of the night, I tossed and turned, analyzing the entire event again and again in my mind. It was a miracle the animal had not charged us at close range, and I could only guess that the wound had been severe enough that the large creature was not strong enough to put up a fight.

We eventually caught up to the buffalo the next day, and my friend was finally able to put it down before dark- but only after the longest follow-up to a wounded animal I have ever undertaken. The buffalo- still in lively shape- had tried returning to the herd, albeit very slowly, with a bullet through the guts and quartering into the liver. Not a flesh wound after all. Although mortally wounded, there was no saying how long before the liver injury would finish the job.

Of course, the noise we heard from the thicket next to where I had carelessly walked the night before was the wounded buffalo. It was in this exact spot that we had picked up his tracks and followed them the next day. We had walked right next to our wounded buffalo in total darkness, and had no idea it was even there. The disaster that could have befallen us that night if we arrived a minute or so later is almost too much to imagine.

Lesson learned: never, ever get too comfortable with a buffalo follow-up. If it's nearing darkness, leave and come back the next day. On the other hand, the other triumph we experienced was to never give up. We had followed the buffalo all day without a hint we were getting closer to the wounded animal. Yet despite our exhaustion- both mentally and physically- we kept on the trail, and our efforts were rewarded at the last possible hour of daylight.

In January 2014, I was a fairly-weathered guide- or at least, I was no beginner. By then, four seasons of guiding were under my belt, full of many buffalo hunts. Some of them, as mentioned, didn't go as planned. Others went without a hitch. But for every mistake made, I worked hard to never repeat the same errors in the proceeding hunts. And for that 2014 hunt, when I found myself following up on a wounded buffalo once again, me and my team were on our best game.

We followed the dark blood, growing increasingly sparse, for the next 300 yards. It took us painful hours even to inch that far. The situation didn't look good. We could tell from the sign that the buffalo had stopped ever-so-often to take his rage out on a small tree, or thrash about in the mud. He was in pain; enough pain to keep him from moving far, but not enough to kill him outright. We were following a very angry buffalo in a thick Congolian lowland forest; perhaps the worst setting to follow a wounded buffalo in.

My client, a very good shot, had hit the animal while it stood broadside next to the forest, just before dark the day before. The buffalo's reaction after the shot was good- as he hunched over with a deep thud upon impact, and there was enough blood to give us assurance that we would find it the next day. But the next day had arrived, and we didn't find a dead buffalo as we had anticipated. Only sparse blood.

All of us- my three trackers, my hunter and myself- were on edge. For over two hours we inched our way forward, expecting at any moment to be met with a charge. But it never came, and soon, I could tell everyone was beginning to let their guards down. This was the sort of moment I knew would inevitably end in disaster; if there's one thing I learned my previous four seasons, its that at the moment you least expect it, things will go wrong.

It took discipline to keep my eyes focused on the wall of greenery in front of me, even while my eyes burned with sweat and blinding sunlight. And just like that, while we all had our noses to the blood trail, I saw a flicker out of my peripheral vision. In a blur, the buffalo was getting to his feet, trying to turn and face us. He never got the chance. I swung around and let my reaction take charge. My first bullet broke the hip, and he lunged forward, only to be met by another bullet- a monolithic solid- through both shoulders. When the buffalo lay still in a cloud of dust, and my ears stopped ringing, I turned around to see the trackers and my hunter looking at me in wide-eyed bewilderment. They later told me they had not even seen the buffalo when I shot.

That evening, we were met with a hero's welcome at the main camp along the Kocho river. The other guests and staff congratulated us on a successful hunt. I didn't celebrate the blissfulness long. A part of learning the ropes of buffalo hunting is understanding your limitations, and not letting success give a false sense of confidence. I knew, despite the celebration, there would be more buffalo hunts to come, and more dangerous follow-ups to be ready for.

Chapter 5: Nature's Classroom

Although my mentorship in the bush took place across vast areas of the Chinko basin- there were two specific regions that stand out as my main classrooms: The thick gallery rainforests of the Mbari river system, where I learned about the forest species and their royal king, the Bongo antelope; and conversely, the dry plateaus between the northern Kocho and Chinko rivers, where I learned about the savanna woodland species and their king, the Lord Derby's eland.

These two types of habitat could not be any more different- and yet, they were often found directly abutting each other. For this reason, species normally endemic to each ecosystem often found themselves interacting with one another- like the time I found a savanna dwelling lion preying on a forest dwelling Giant Forest hog. This is what makes the eastern Central African Republic so unique.

RAINFOREST

Early in my apprenticeship, I spent much of my time working out of our Mbari river camp. This camp was situated next to where our road crossed this river, which allowed access to the rest of the hunting block. Because the ferry crossing here required a lot of maintenance every year after the rainy season (a job that inevitably fell on me), necessity forced me to spend a lot of time exploring this area and developing it for hunting purposes.

From camp, all around us loomed dark, foreboding forests. Black and white Colobus monkeys jumped in the high canopy above, unseen except for the violent shaking of the branches. Almost every evening we heard leopard letting out their guttural, engine revving calls. And occasionally, when the forest always seemed the most still- the screaming wail of a tree hyrax would disrupt the silence, unnerving us.

As menacing as the forest seemed looking at it from the outside- it took on the feeling of a shelter once we entered the dense canopy to escape the heat of the day. At first, walking in the forest was a challenge with my tall, upright American gate, and I was always getting my boots stuck on unseen roots and tumbling face-first into the mud. But once I mimicked the African's gate- which required a more relaxed, intuitive flow of the feet and eyes in coordination- moving through the thick forest became more comfortable.

Trying to describe a tropical forest is as challenging as describing the ocean to those who have never been: to the inexperienced eye, there seems to be no details to the sea of green. And then, through slow assimilation by being in the environment, one begins to notice the nuanced layers of the landscape. Eventually, those subtle nuances become striking characteristics.

The "standard" forests of the Chinko basin consist of large trees as tall as buildings scattered every 20-30 yards or so, with knee-high undergrowth carpeting the entire ground. Walking in such forests is relatively easy, and visibility might be 50-100 yards. Other forests, usually lower in elevation and often along water drainages, are much thicker. Walking here requires slashing every few steps with a machete to clear a path. This is truly thick, with visibility down to 5 yards. Trees vary in size from tall primary rainforest trees, down to short trees that are little taller than a man. Lianas, vines, and nettles wrap themselves around everything, creating a nearly impenetrable wall of green. Pushing through 1 mile of such forest might take three hours. And then, there are swampy forests that at first appear like any other forests, until one suddenly finds themselves sinking into knee-high muddy water. Glossy leaves the size of traffic signs cover the ground, concealing hidden roots and puddles.

Our machetes were our main tools in the forest. At first, I hacked the vines and saplings in front of me wildly- but the foliage simply bounced away from the strikes. The problem was my stroke came from a direct side-swing. The Africans showed me their technique, which required a sharp diagonal down-swing. It took me years to master the technique, and by my last season as a PH, some of the new African staff marveled at my proficiency with the machete.

Among my company were local hunters who were experienced in these very forests. I took every moment I could to enlist these men to take me out for some exploring. I always masked these personal excursions under the guise of cutting new hunting trails or discovering new bongo salt-licks to take future clients to.

One of my favorite forests to explore was just a few miles north of our camp. The forest edge started on top of a plateau, but once we entered the trees, the geography changed drastically, and dropped down into a steep canyon bowl, like a crater. All around us, cliff-faces walled us in. Inside the bowl were a series of spring fed creeks starting from or leading to numerous salt-licks visited by bongo, buffalo, forest pigs- and in years past- elephant.

The first time we came here we had no set mission or plan, we just explored at our own leisure and hunted for duikers as we went. That first day, we called in blue duiker and the rusty-red Weyns' duiker; species we expected to find there. However, I was not expecting to call in a Bay duiker, since the species was not known to exist this far east- but that's just what we did in a small grove of feral lemon trees. Later, we called in a loud and aggressive Yellow-backed duiker- the largest duiker species in these parts. It sounded like a freight train ripping through the trees at it came rushing in, only to turn immediately in fright after scenting us.

As we climbed out of the steep canyon cliffs that afternoon using tree roots and branches for support, I looked to my left and noticed the entrance to a small cave. Carefully navigating sideways, I peered into the cave. I switched on a flashlight and nearly stumbled backwards as a roost of bats came fluttering out. Fortunately, not all of the bats had escaped, and I was delighted to see a handful of them resting upside-down inside the cave, looking at me groggily.

Later, we would come back to this forest and cut a series of foot paths penetrating straight through it. The animal encounters were unnumerable: one night, while camped close by, I accompanied some of the men on a night hunt for duiker. We hadn't made it far from our camp when the hunt was cut short after we blundered into a cantankerous hippopotamus moving slowly and noisily through the forest in pitch darkness. Later, I had one of my earliest encounters with a group of Giant Forest hogs here, which came ripping across my front when I disturbed them in the low-growth along a spring-fed creek. One day, while following a footpath to a salt-lick where bongo frequented, I was shocked to find on my return down the same foot-path, a set of fresh leopard tracks following mine. Rounding a bend in the trail a few minutes later, I came face-to-face with the young cat itself before it bounded away in fright.

In the mud and soft-soil, I was taught how to identify the tracks of all the forest species: the small spade shaped track of the Yellow-backed duiker and the similar but slightly sharper track of the bushbuck; the round-edged elk-like track of the bongo antelope, and the stocky, feline track of the elusive Golden cat. On heavily used game trails, I set up cheap camera traps, and was rewarded with images of these elusive animals that called the forest home.

One afternoon, I was coming down the creek-bed where the game trails converged in order to check the camera traps, not paying attention to where I was going, I stumbled upon a ghastly sight that took me a moment to fully process: a huge African rock python, perhaps 14 feet in length, lay stretched out in the shallow water, with its mouth distended to unbelievable proportions, halfway through devouring a full-grown bushbuck female. The men with me begged me to allow them to kill the snake, but I refused. I hastened us to leave the snake alone and not disturb it, but it was too late- the snake was clearly alarmed by the gawking men, and quickly ejected the bushbuck; a meal that no doubt had taken the animal many days to procure. Alas, when the snake had retired unseen into the leafy forest floor, I made a compromise with the men and let them steal the unlucky snake's bushbuck meal. The very idea of eating meat that had been in the mouth of the serpent was enough to make me gag, and I politely declined the invitation to join the feast later that night in camp.

In the fall of 2010, while stationed at the Mbari camp, my attachment to the forest here became much more intimate when an unseasonable rainstorm swept through, causing mudslides which blocked the roads to and from our camp. For a week we were stranded here with no resupply of rations. We resorted to killing baboons and monkeys to feed us, and when this became unbearable to the palate, we set off in small groups and foraged in the forest. We found edible mushrooms, nuts, vines, leaves, bland fruits- and even wild yams the size of a man's calf. In this way, my education in this rainforest classroom moved beyond the academic and into the practical.

In time, I would grow comfortable with hunting around camp alone. Whenever we needed fresh meat for our work, I would stalk the edges of the deeper forests. Sometimes my take would be Crested guinea fowl or baboons. Other times, it would be blue duiker. I got quite good at calling in the duikers like my African companions had taught me, with the nasally mouth calls that required pinching my nose and pushing my lips outwards while making a mooing sound. I also grew an eye for knowing just what good blue duiker habitat looked like- although I couldn't describe it in words today; it was an instinctual knowledge that I gained from hours spent hunting them. Whenever I came upon a spot, I would call out into the dark green abyss, and almost always be answered by the approach of the mystical little beast.

SAVANNA

My mentorship in the dry, woodland savanna plateaus of Giant eland country started under more blunt circumstances. During my first-year apprenticeship, while I was busy driving around and inspecting area salt-licks for animal activity, Erik called me out of the blue on my satellite phone and instructed me to grab a rucksack with food for a few days and meet him at a designated GPS coordinate an hour's drive away. Without question, I set off to meet him.

It was late in the afternoon when I found Erik's hunting truck parked under some thin shade high on a dry plateau along the Chinko river. His overweight American client was lying half-dead in the elevated observation seat of the Land Cruiser, with a big sun hat covering his open-mouthed face. Erik got straight to the point, speaking low enough so the client couldn't hear him.

"We've been following a herd of eland all day and haven't been able to get close," he said. "This yank is never going to get an eland if he has to track them for another full day."

I already knew in that moment what Erik intended. Two African trackers stood ready by Erik's side.

"I need you to follow Mohomet and his cousin," he said gesturing to the Africans. "They will track the eland tomorrow- and if necessary, the next day. When the animals cross a road, I want you to call me immediately. Hopefully, the client will be rested enough that we can continue the pursuit straight from the road."

With little more sentiment than this brief instruction, Erik climbed onto his truck and disappeared with his client in a cloud of dust.

"Let's go," Mohomet hissed, before I even had time to fully strap my backpack on. We were off on the trail of the Giant eland.

We wove in and out of the rusty brown woodland with scattered Mopani trees and Monkey-fruit trees; species evolved specifically to handle the seasonal fires that sweep through the area. This particular spot was burned only a few weeks prior. Black ash clung to the small trees; only surface level scars covering their unburnt interior. Fresh green grass sprouted about an inch out of the black earth, painting the ground in splashes of contrasting dark blacks and bright greens.

Just like the forests, to the untrained eye, the savanna woodlands appear like one undiscernible patch of drab-colored grass and thicket. But after walking long enough, one begins to notice the nuances to the landscape. Thickets of dry forests- including wild coffee trees- stand out like scattered islands atop small openings of black, lateric stone ground where no plants taller than grass can grow. Between these rise small thickets of short, woodland trees. At first, the landscape seems devoid of life. And then, one immediately notices a constant flow of grey hornbill birds fluttering in and out of the trees, hunting insects. Olive monkeys, Patas monkeys and baboons can appear at any moment, silently slinking around the grassy foliage. Game densities are low here, but occasionally, the less-common larger mammals like roan, Lelwel hartebeest, western kob and waterbuck make their appearance.

    Mohomet was supposedly following the tracks of a herd of eland- but on the dry ground scattered with leaves and small rocks, I saw absolutely no hint of their passing. I tried in vain to see what he saw- but for the moment, I was left to simply trust his judgment and stay behind him.

    After awhile, my eyes began to adjust slowly, and I could make out perfectly outlined tracks appearing in small patches of sandy soil. Then, I noted piles of eland droppings on the ground. I scooped some up in my fingers and squeezed, but they were crunchy and brittle- and not what I expected fresh dropping to look like.

    "These don't look very fresh to me," I said to Mahomet, prompting an irritated snort from him.

    "You will see," he assured me with a hint of annoyance in his voice.

At some point, we found where the herd had stopped at a small pool to drink a few hours before. The creek had begun to dry out since the rainy season ended two months prior, and only a few scattered pools of water remained. Mohomet and his cousin squatted down to refill their water bottles. I looked down at the cloudy, stagnant water and hesitated. My bottle was nearly empty, but the water before me looked suspect. I slowly scooped some up before adding a couple tablets of iodine. Mohomet, observing this, scoffed at me again.

"White men's stomachs are weak," he laughed, and I did not protest this assessment.

We briefly entertained the idea of continuing further, but with darkness quickly approaching and finding ourselves near the only pools of water we had seen all day, we decided to make camp for the night. We set up a crude fire next to a small pool of water and lay our sleeping mats right on the ground. Soon, two soot-blackened cooking pots were placed on the fire- one with rice, and the other with coffee. By the time dinner was ready, the sun was only a sliver on the horizon. Luckily, we were high enough on the dry plateaus of the Chinko basin that the mosquitos weren't too bad.

Mohomet sat shirtless next to the fire, a leather pouch tied to a necklace dangled across his chest- concealing magical amulets and talismans meant to protect him from evil spirits. The charms were also meant to protect him from dangers in the bush- which to the men, were always directly tied to evil spirits. His light-brown skin glistened with sweat. His eyes flashed sharply and hinted of reposed firry aggression. He expressed many times his dislike for privileged white people; however, the more time I spent roughing it in the bush, the more he revealed his rare approval of me.

That night, Mohomet regaled us with stories of his elephant hunting adventures. Though many of the Africans living in this frontier of the Central African Republic were proficient hunters- few of them could call themselves "elephant hunters," a title Mohomet proudly owned. He described his hunt for the mammoth-like creatures deep in the forest around the Mbari. The real test of a man's courage, he said, was crawling into the dense brush to confront the animals up close and personal, and then standing your ground when the shooting started.

He described one hunt in particular.

"By the time we reached within shooting distance of the animals in a small forest stream, they had already begun to smell us and were nervous," he said. "An older hunter in front of me started shooting, and as the lead elephant dropped, many more came charging at us."

"Everyone scattered, even the experienced hunters, and only I stood my ground there in a small clearing, exposed to the fleeing animals," he said proudly. "I waited until the very last second as a bull came charging in, and I sent one perfectly placed bullet through its head, dropping it at my feet."

The story could have been an exaggeration, but from the stories I had heard from other hunters who had accompanied Mohomet on his *grande chasse* hunts- I knew it was not.

The stars shone bright above the few scattered trees in our dry creek-bed home for the night. The high plateau of the savanna woodland was even more silent at night than the rainforests, which gave a timeless and eerie feeling to the place. I felt privileged to be there with that man and share company with him, to hear his stories and glimpse a more ancient world that is becoming more and more rare in the 21st Century. As we drifted off to sleep around the campfire, it was impossible for me to know in that moment, that in a few years' time- Mohomet would be killed by UN peacekeeping soldiers defending a field hospital in Bangassou as he raided it with a group of his fellow "Anti-Balaka" rebels attempting to execute wounded faction rebel fighters there during the impending Civil War. Alas, these were all events still in the making.

The next day we wasted no time in following the eland again at the first start of daylight. The animals moved even farther away from the last pools of water in the dry creek beds and took us straight into a labyrinth of rocky hills. The thirst was becoming acute when we started noticing dry, powdery white vines hanging on acacia and Monkey-fruit trees. These vines, when cut at both ends, release a thick, sappy-tasting water. While Mohomet and his cousin occasionally slashed a section to drink, I was continuously slashing every one I came across, gluttonously drinking what I could.

At one point in a saddle between two rocky hills, we found the fresh pug marks of a pair of lions in the sandy ground. None of us had weapons for which to defend ourselves, apart from our machetes, and I looked around with renewed caution. Just a few weeks before, Anton and his clients had seen a group of three feisty juvenile lions devouring an eland carcass not far from the spot.

As the day progressed, Mohomet was growing increasingly excited about the prospects of catching up to the large eland herd. The sign, he said, was very fresh. Again, I reached down and squished the droppings between my fingers, and they only seemed slightly softer than the dry droppings we had seen the day before. When we came across leaves that had been chewed by the animals, I inspected these too, trying to get a sense for how quickly such sign dries in the hot sun. It was difficult to stay motivated and vigilant during the long walk. Mohomet's seemingly boundless energy only grew stronger as we came across the fresh animal sign.

I was half-delirious with heat, barely keeping my eyes from the ground immediately in front of me, when Mohomet hissed and pulled me to the ground.

"Bozobo!" he whispered (the name for eland in Sango).

Right next to us, on a small ridge flanking our own ridge less than a hundred yards away- the mythical eland appeared like an enigma, moving parallel to us. Their tan hides blended perfectly with the earthen colored trees of the Sudan-Guinean woodland, and if not for the erratic flicker of tails and twitching of ears, I probably would have still missed them. After tracking them unseen for two days, their sudden appearance felt almost unreal.

Two years later, at the age of 21, I would successfully guide my first Lord Derby's eland hunt in this very place. In that time, it would take 12 of the 14 days for us to finally put our hands on the elusive antelope's 51-inch spiral horns. I remember thinking it was a dream- an impossible fantasy- to finally be able to touch the sweet musky smelling animal after so many miles of hard work.

After the animals moved past us, the excited Mohomet instructed me to call Erik. I looked down at my GPS and noted the road just ahead of us. I quickly rang Erik on the satellite phone, and we waited an hour there for him to arrive with the client. As it was now evening, the animals were taking advantage of the cooler temperatures and had stopped to feed. Miraculously, they had not seen or smelled us that entire time. When Erik and the overweight American got there, it was only a matter of the men following Mahomet for a quarter of a mile and then picking out the large herd bull before shooting.

When I arrived at the small clearing where the eland lay, I found the proud American posing behind the animal triumphantly, snapping trophy photos. He pulled out a tape measure and began obsessively measuring the animal's horns- wondering if they would make it into the SCI trophy book, or more importantly- if they were larger horns than the ones his hunting partner in camp had secured with Anton a few days before.

As the man was celebrating his big proud hunting accomplishment- the real hunter stood quietly in a corner smoking a cigarette in tattered clothes, receiving less than a simple thank you. So I walked up to Mohemet myself, and thanked him for teaching me the ways of the *bozobo*. By sharing his knowledge, I was able to walk in the footsteps and sleep on the ground behind the most impressive antelope on earth.

Chapter 6: The Bushbuck

In October 2010, I found myself a second-year apprentice PH stationed at the muddy Mbari river. I was here to oversee the work of two large groups of local African men; one strengthening our vehicle ferry on the river, and the other, cutting a network of small hunting trails in the forest.

One day, I set off with a couple ex-poachers who had told me about a salt-lick deep in the forest frequented by many animals. We followed a barely discernable game trail through dry forest, eventually climbing down into a muddy swamp. In the swamps, I looked eagerly but in vain for the tracks of the elusive forest sitatunga. Even more frequent than bongo tracks, were endless amounts of bushbuck tracks.

The Harnessed bushbuck is the subspecies of bushbuck found in this part of Central Africa. It is a beautiful animal I like to refer to as the miniature bongo. Small in size compared to other bushbuck species, where they lack in a large body, they make up for in brilliant colors. Their base color is a bright orange-red, with vivid white spots and stripes down its flanks, with a few horizontal white stripes across its back side. Some of the males even have dark black spots on their legs. The mature animals lose the thin hair around their shoulder up to their head, leaving a charcoal-colored neck and face. Like all other bushbuck sub-species, the Harnessed bushbuck is an unbelievably elegant animal.

As a second-year apprentice, I was not allowed to shoot any animal for meat except for "small game" -like duikers, baboon, and guinea fowl. For nearly two weeks in our remote camp along the river, we had lived chiefly off *gozo* (dough-like manioc root), and baboon meat- simply because the grass was still too high to allow for hunting. I resisted eating the meat for as long as I could, until my hunger won over.

I found baboon meat to not be so inedible, though after many days of eating an animal with human-like features, I was beginning to grow weary of the diet. With much work left and many mouths to feed before the grass was dry enough to burn, my boss Erik finally relented and gave me the green light to shoot other, larger species. He told me if I came across a good buffalo bull, warthog, or bushbuck, I could take one for meat.

Of course, after many days of seeing bushbuck around every bend, once I was given permission to hunt them, the animals vanished into thin air.

Back in the forest, on our way to the salt-lick, it was clear the animals were in abundance here, and I eagerly expected to meet one at any moment. We never did, but the journey that day was amazing none-the-less. We had the opportunity to scout a forest that was previously unexplored. The salt-lick, when we arrived there, proved to be a bongo and bushbuck paradise. At that time of the year, it was still quite swampy from recent rains. In addition to lots of promising hoofed animal sign, we also found various python ruts intersecting the mud.

We marked the salt-lick on our GPS, and then sat down for a lunch break. We did not have any meat, but instead one of the men had brought along *gozo* and homemade peanut butter his wife had sent him from the closest village about 120 miles away by road. After lunch, we set off on our back trail, and made it to our Mbari camp by evening.

The climate of the equatorial Central African Republic is characterized by very cool mornings and evening, and blazing hot midday temperatures. Many of the animals here can be patterned quite accurately depending on these daytime temperatures. For example, buffalo feed prolifically in the morning and evening, but sleep during most of the heat of the day. Eland walk endlessly in the morning and evening, but walk and feed intermediately throughout the heat of the day. Almost all species can be successfully stalked and hunted primarily in the morning and evening.

In other words, its safe to say that once the sun comes up around 10am and on toward 3pm, most animals become scarce. The exception to this rule (apart from the pig species that can be hunted at any time), is the Harnessed bushbuck. In my opinion, both the bushbuck and the Giant Forest hog are the least predictable animals in regard to daily temperatures. Both can show up in the most unexpected circumstances, in the hottest part of the day, for no apparent rhyme or reason. Usually though, the bushbuck will still stay in somewhat shady spots, in tall grass or along the forest edge.

I have seen bushbuck materialize on large salt-licks in soaring mid-day temps countless times. I have found, the perfect strategy to hunting them in this landscape characterized by scattered forests and open woodland, is to focus on the edge of forested streams during the morning, and then cool stream beds and calm forest salt-licks during the heat of the day. Because of this habit of theirs to be active during times most other animals are sleeping, a hunter can make the most of their time by focusing on tracking eland and buffalo during the morning and evening, and then spend time looking for bushbuck during the middle of the day; thus utilizing all available daylight for hunting.

The Harnessed bushbuck can be at many times the wild card of hunting in these parts. You can exhaust all effort in searching for the animal and may never find him. You might also be searching tirelessly for another species, and find bushbuck trophies behind every bush. The lesson here for the traveling hunter is to never pass up an unexpected opportunity at this unique trophy.

On one safari I participated in, my hunter and I had pursued eland for two days. He had previously told me his keen desire to take a Harnessed bushbuck. Knowing this, and knowing we had almost two full weeks to pursue eland, I suggested he take the bushbuck male that suddenly appeared on the trail of the eland herd we were pursuing. The hunter did not hesitate, and with the shot, the day of eland hunting was ruined- but a bushbuck was on the ground- and for the rest of the safari, proved to be the only bushbuck male we would encounter.

On another safari, a hunter friend and I were in a high-stand overlooking a salt-lick deep in the forest in pursuit of bongo. With the hours of his final hunting day winding down, we were getting anxious to make something happen. Just as we were about to call it a day and leave, movement down below in a patch of swampy grass caught our attention. After some agonizing minutes trying to make out the identity of the animal, a huge old trophy Harnessed bushbuck slowly materialized out of the grass. My American friend did not hesitate at the opportunity. And although no bongo materialized on the salt-lick for the final morning of the hunt, the old bushbuck male with polished horns was a rare trophy that sent him home satisfied.

Going back to my story- a few days after we had first visited the bushbuck salt-lick near the Mbari river, a couple Africans and I were following a stream bed leading toward the opening of the forest in an attempt to find a good tree for which to build a high-stand overlooking the salt-lick. On a rise, one of the Africans in front of me spotted something downhill, moving through the dense forest. Raising my binoculars, I soon made out the white spots and stripes of a bushbuck. Alas, after breaking apart the bush with my binoculars, I discovered it was only a small female. She was moving toward the salt-lick. Now, on full vigil, we slowly followed the animal tracks leading to the salt-lick.

It was now the heat of the day, and the forest was deathly quiet. We slowly left the dark forest and emerged onto the edge of the brilliantly-lit salt-lick. Suddenly, we made out two black horns on a red neck sticking above the long grass in a swampy section of the opening. Everyone dropped to the ground instantly. Taking a moment to regain my nerves, I quietly chambered a round in my rifle and began crawling to the left to flank the animal. At about 80 yards, with no solid rest and only grass to conceal me, I rose to my knees and put the scope on the bushbuck. He was a decent male- not old or a huge trophy, but a mature animal. I slowly pulled the trigger on the old .30-06 and sent a bullet through both shoulders.

After only hunting small game for the last two years, it was overwhelming walking up to the beautiful bushbuck- my first real African trophy. It was one of those surreal moments in my hunting career, when I stopped to look at the exotic animal and the lushes tropical forest surrounding, and thought to myself, *is this reality? Had I not just been in my homeland in Kansas, hunting Whitetail deer in small woodlots?*

Elated by the experience, I quickly quartered the buck and lashed half the meat onto a large sapling and carried it across my shoulders. Another African took the other half of the meat on his shoulders, and the two of us staggered up the steep, muddy forest trail and to the road 1.5 miles away. I was panting heavily and soaked in sweat when we got to our small fly camp along the Mbari, with stars stretched fully across the sky. While the African staff was alive and vibrant as ever, celebrating the prospects of having delicious meat for the first time in many days, I fell into easy sleep, blissful from a full day's hunting adventure, and watched the red and white stripes of the miniature bongo cousin dance across my dreams.

Chapter 7: The Rookie and the Giant Roan

On the road to becoming a Professional Hunter, I was told time and time again that a good PH did not just need to possess good hunting skills- but they also needed to have good people skills, good management skills, solid mechanical knowledge- and most important of all, be a good showman. In this last category, I was certainly no master, but in the brief moments when my reputation was in dire risk, the necessity to save my own skin forced me to draw upon my shrewdest resources.

Take for example, the third safari I ever guided- when I was still technically an apprentice. It was a two-week hunt for buffalo and Roan antelope. And my client- a frugal old blue collard American- wanted to kill exactly those two animals: a Roan and a buffalo.

The buffalo came easily enough- almost suspiciously easy. During the two previous safaris, I had had to work hard as a novice to achieve success, spending many miles and days in pursuit of our quarry before connecting. But on this hunt, everything fell into place that first morning.

We tracked the herd until we found them at their first bedding area of the day, perched under a lone tree on top of a hill overlooking a beautiful valley. The animals were easy to spot as they were silhouetted against the drab skyline. And as further luck, the big herd bull was laying closets to us. When I pointed the animal out to the client, he rested his rifle on my shooting sticks, took aim, and fired. Whether by luck or on purpose- the bull fell dead instantly, with the large .416 Remington severing its spinal cord at the base of the neck.

Now, the pressure was on to secure a Roan antelope.

I do not know what it is like hunting Roan antelope in other parts of Africa, but in the Chinko basin, it was dauntingly difficult. Tracking the animals was nearly impossible, as their senses were so acute, and they would run without stopping once they realized they were being followed. Their population density was also low in the region, so intentionally seeking them out to hunt was practically unrealistic. And at that point in my career, I had never hunted one before. In fact, I had only ever seen a few of the regal, horse-like antelope in all my time in the bush.

Roan sightings were always brief, like the time I bumped into a lone male while cutting a road, and watched his backwards curved horns rise and fall above the long grass like sickles as it ran. Or the other time, I happened to turn my head to the side of my vehicle as I drove, and watched as a herd of Roan galloped parallel to me, weaving in and out of the trees of a dry Mopani woodland in flashes, like ghosts.

These sightings were always random and unexpected, and I had no idea how or where to replicate such encounters with a client intentionally seeking the animals to hunt. That is, except for the "airport salt-lick," an exposed mineral lick near our bush airstrip on the Kocho river plateau, where a couple herds of the antelope were (somewhat) consistently spotted. Going off of this knowledge alone, I began to stake out this specific salt-lick religiously for the remainder of the safari.

We would drive the road where the salt-lick was located, and park the truck a few hundred yards away before carefully approaching on foot. Sometimes, we would even sit behind a clump of trees overlooking the salt-lick, and have a slow lunch in the hopes of ambushing the animals. Always, we would find the fresh tracks of the antelope on the salt-lick, but never managed to catch them. Though we saw this sign often, up to then, the client had yet to see a Roan antelope his entire safari. It felt like the animals were taunting us.

One brisk morning, while bundled up in warm layers, we decided to leave earlier than usual to check out the airport salt-lick.

We parked the truck and headed toward the salt-lick on foot like we had thus far done a dozen times. But on this particular morning, something felt different, and the air was charged with electric energy. Anticipation boiled over as we neared the final rise before the salt-lick spread out before us. I hissed at the client and trackers to slow down in order to catch our breaths and compose ourselves. Then, as carefully as I dared, I crawled forward over the rise where I finally had a clear view of the mineral lick, 150 yards away.

There, standing proudly leading its harem, was the biggest Roan antelope my novice eyes had ever seen. I tried to steady my shaking limbs as I slowly set up the shooting sticks and gently pushed the client forward, instructing him to shoot.

It was only a brief moment in which the client took aim and I covered my ears awaiting the shot- but the animals suddenly noticed us, and that brief delay was about all my nerves could handle. The hunter pulled the trigger, and the big Roan dropped stone dead.

As we approached the fallen animal, the rest of the herd lingered there confused, reluctant to leave. It was only when we were a few feet away that the other animals got the message and tore away in a cloud of dust. As I stooped down to examine the creature, the hunter and trackers stood behind me singing and laughing in celebration. But something gave me pause. As I squatted down, I realized just what it was.

The horns of the animal were indeed large- the largest I had ever seen. But something about the creature's face didn't look right. And then, I noticed the large udder laying limp between the animal's legs- and everything became clear. My stomach dropped. *We had killed a female.*

My mind raced trying to come up with something to say to the client. It would only be a matter of time before he too noticed the problem. I had to come up with a solution fast. Should I be honest straight away and tell him? Or risk looking like a fool by not mentioning the mistake, despite what his own eyes would surely tell him? Before I could even say anything, a painful, unexpected play of fate intervened to save the day.

"Ouch!" the client screamed, and I turned to find him swapping a bee that had just stung him in the neck. Suddenly, I felt an explosion of pain on my ear. We were under attack by a swarm of angry bees!

Immediately, I took advantage of the blessed distraction and screamed at the hunter to retreat. A hundred yards away we stopped running and rested under a tree, panting like dogs. We made a big fire and cut down dozens of leafy branches and threw them on the flames to create smoke to fend off the angry insects. I instructed the client to stay there while we finished skinning the animal. It was the perfect excuse to keep his eyes off the carcass. With a freshly glowing set of embers, we advanced onto the kill site and made our own fire there to ward off the bees.

The trackers were snickering and poking the animal's udder, but I scolded them harshly under my breath in Sango.

"He doesn't know it's a female!" I said. "If we can keep him away while we skin it, maybe he won't find out."

With these instructions, the men returned to their work in silence, quickly and diligently getting the animal quartered and skinned. Soon, all evidence of the animal's sex was tossed into the bushes and quickly covered in bees- which were attracted to the mineral-rich blood. While we worked, the client was busy nursing the painful bee stings on his face and neck, and he needed no further convincing to stay away. It seemed as if I had gotten away with my blunder.

As we arrived in camp, we were met with a throng of camp staff singing and dancing in celebration. My boss, Erik Mararv, also greeted us there with a smile. As the Toyota truck stopped just in front of him, he peered in the back where the Roan horns protruded, and glanced down for a split second at the trophy before turning back to the client, nodding his head approvingly.

"Well done!" he said patting the man on his back, "This truly is an exceptional animal for this area!"

By his reaction, I knew in that moment I had not only fooled the client, I had also fooled my boss.

The trackers left us to continue our celebration at the dining area, while they took the skull and skin to be treated by the company taxidermist. We had a hearty dinner with the client next to the bubbling black Kocho river, as the sun went down and the stars rose to pepper the sky. The client was thoroughly exhausted by the day's events, and bid us an early goodnight before retiring to his bungalow a short distance away.

Just the two of us now, Erik suddenly grew sentimental and drew closer, offering me a cold beer before taking one himself. He observed me for a moment, with a rare twinkle in his eye. And for a brief second, I almost felt guilty about deceiving him.

"Cheers," he said, clanking his bottle to mine, "You truly are a gifted guide."

I looked down, embarrassed by the complement, and wondered if I should tell him the truth.

"I mean…" he continued, "you'd have to be a good guide to be able to shoot a fucking female Roan and convince your client it's the biggest bull you've ever seen."

I looked up and found him grinning at me devilishly.

Postscript:

Although I make light of this story now many years later, the incident was not something I took lightly at the time. Intentionally killing a female of any species is illegal in the Central African Republic. However, there were protocols for genuine mistakes- as was the case here- which resulted in penalties. In this case, shooting the female Roan ended up costing us more than double the standard trophy fee, which Erik graciously covered. My readers might forgive me of this mistake if they consider this was my first season guiding. It was also the first and only time I ever mistakenly killed a female of any species while on safari. More embarrassing, we eventually had to tell the client about my mistake, but the man was gracious and understanding. Considering how big the horns were- and how indistinguishable they were to a male's- he was just as happy to display them in his trophy room.

Chapter 8: Picking a Fight

Growing up, my older brother and I were always picked on by bullies due to our small size, but this didn't stop us from standing up for ourselves. Though we were small, we often found ourselves getting into violent fist fights with older boys. Our father, who was also bullied as a kid, didn't discourage us from fighting back; in fact, he encouraged it, as long as we followed one rule of engagement: never be the person to pick a fight, but only act in self-defense when someone else starts it. He reasoned that if we followed this rule, even if we lost, at least there would be no shame in failing. But if, on the other hand, we started the fight and then lost, we would rightfully carry the shame of the defeat.

It is no surprise then that I felt more than a little hesitant when I began "picking fights" with animals in Africa. You see, I learned to employ a series of traditional hunting methods unique to Central Africa that required intentionally angering certain species in order to draw them in closer for a confrontation.

We picked fights with buffalo, we picked fights with territorial forest duikers, *and we even picked fights with lions*. We did this by using a variety of calls to attract the animals to us- either while mimicking a fellow member in distress, or a territorial challenge. But just like picking a fist-fight in my childhood, there was something unsettling about picking these hunting fights. It went against every instinct in my bones to boldly announce my presence to an animals that would normally be approached by stealth.

And yet, the better I got at it, the more exciting it became to pick a fight. Especially for forest duikers.

One of the most well-known methods for hunting the numerous duiker species in the thick equatorial rainforests of Africa is the use of a nasally nose call. I and many others have written about this- but to summarize: one presses their nose flat while pushing their lips up and out, and then letting out a high-pitched mooing sound. This is a traditional method used throughout Central Africa from many tribes- including the famous pygmies.

The secretive nature of the forest duikers made calling them into close range even more rewarding. The Yellow-backed duiker, for example, was a persistent ghost in the riverine forests of the Chinko basin. Their presence was known by the many tracks we found, but sightings of them in the flesh were maddeningly rare. One could go months romping through the bush without seeing them, and then, stopping for a brief pause in a random patch of bush, a caller would summon them from the bowels of the forest. And there, the ghost would stand, a shotguns distance away, eyes bulging and muscles twitching with curious attention.

I became very good at calling in the smaller blue duikers. The larger duikers- like the Yellow-backed- were only successfully called by the most skilled callers. And some secretive species, like the Bay duiker- were even more rarely called into range, even by the most experienced callers.

Despite their small size, the hunt for the duiker would amount to one of the most exciting endeavors in the bush. It felt like casting a spell into an enchanted forest and bringing forth all its strange creatures. The caller would creep slowly through the undergrowth, and at a suitable spot would stop, and then let out the squealing call. Often, the first few calls would be met with silence; but then, out of nowhere, the forest would erupt with the sound of greenery ripping apart, as a territorial duiker would come thumping toward the sound of the call. When approaching a call, the blue duikers would sound as loud as bushbuck; and the even larger Yellow-backed duikers would sound like buffalo.

What made this method of hunting even more exciting, was the added variable of possibly calling in other, more predatory species by mistake.

Although neither I nor anyone else I knew had successfully called in lion during a duiker hunt, I am certain it is still a possibility, considering the amount of lion that would later show up on camera traps in the rainforest.

Once, while hunting with a client in a relatively large forest covered in dry leaves, my lead tracker, Charles, was calling loudly for duikers, when he suddenly stopped. I looked at his face and could tell from his furrowed brows of concentration that something was troubling him. I listened too, and soon found myself hearing the same disturbance. Faintly, at a distance that could have been far away or very close (no one could say for certain), we began to hear something creeping toward us.

Try as I may, my eyes could not break apart the foliage in front of me enough to be able to see what was approaching. I turned to Charles again, and his eyes suddenly widened in shock. In the same instant, the form of a leopard materialized from its flattened position just in front of us before turning and exploding away.

The shock sent Charles stumbling backwards and I behind him.

"Ze la!" he shrieked in Sango. "My god that was close!"

I turned to the old client behind me, who was still furrowing his brows, clearly still unable to make out what had just happened in front of him. When I explained that a leopard had just snuck up on us, the man refused to believe it.

But accidentally calling a leopard in doesn't compare to the thrill of intentionally calling in the king of beasts.

My experience hunting lions is limited to a single safari I partook in as an apprentice. And just like with many of our hunting methods in the thick bush of the Chinko basin, this hunt also required "picking a fight."

With a long, cone-shaped horn made of sheet metal and wrapped in animal hide, we learned to call lions in from long distances (a tradition that was widely used in Central Africa but has not taken on in other regions of Africa). We used this instrument to let out the bellowing grunts the animals are famous for. Though people mistakenly call this a "roar," its really a series of deep moans that start off loud and then descend in increasingly quieter repetitions.

We had to use this method out of necessity to attract the animals, because the environment was so thick, spotting lions in the flesh was difficult. Encountering them often occurred by chance while we pursued other creatures. When preparing for a lion hunt, we sometimes hung buffalo carcasses as bait in areas we knew were frequented by lions, in the hopes of keeping them in the area long enough for the arrival of the client, but this yielded mixed results.

We only conducted one or two lion hunts each season. We received a handful of licenses each year from the game department, but due to our own estimated population size- we opted to be very conservative about our lion harvests, and always shot way less than we were allowed. During my very first season in Africa, I was invited to join in on a lion hunt in a small way.

The client was a wealthy Luxemburgish man who only had a week to hunt. When he arrived, we were frantic to locate a lion. That first night, Erik sent me alone with one of our lion horns to call into the darkness in the hopes of locating some cats; he then went in another direction to call with the client. I had only recently started practicing the lion call after Anton, Erik's childhood friend and fellow Swede, had shown me. I was nervous about making a bad sounding call and risk scaring away the lions, but I decided to go for it anyway. I drove through the cool dark night, my headlights cutting into the bush before I located a suitable spot on a hill. There, I stopped the car, turned off the engine, and in an instant- the darkness of the night swallowed me up.

I climbed on top of the truck and got in position with the large metal call. I reasoned that I needed to be elevated to better project the noise across the savanna woodlands. But in reality, I did it because I was terrified of being inside the open cab. The air was cold, and I threw on a jacket out of necessity. I waited there alone in the silence for a long moment, hesitant to even move, carefully listening for any sound in the bush around me. I was half afraid that the instant I let loose on the horn, the bush around me would erupt with roaring lions. Instead, when I did let out the loud, mournful bellows- an even eerier silence smothered the bush when the calling ceased.

I called in intervals for a long time. As I loosed the roaring into the sky, the now blackened landscape began to lose all ties to time and space. My calls were sent into an ancient, primordial landscape, and as far as I knew in that moment- I could have been summoning a mythical beast; perhaps even a saber toothed tiger.

This went on for a long time, and just before I began to shift around anxiously, I stopped dead still: off in the distance, faint to the point of almost being inaudible, I heard the soft vibrations of a lion calling in the distance. I held my breath and listened long enough to confirm what I was hearing. And then, silence.

I waited for a long time, barely breathing, hoping to hear the roaring again. But nothing stirred. It was already late, and I decided that the lion had been calling out of pure coincidence and not responding to my call.

I headed back to camp and got there long after Erik and the client had gone to bed, and so was unable to inform them of the night's events. But it did not matter, for the next day, just as the camp was stirring, Erik and the client drove out and encountered a male lion courting a female not far away. Even before we heard the shot, we could hear the lions roaring in the distance, and we knew they were close. When the shot did reach our ears, we knew it could only mean one thing.

At the first random spot the hunters stopped at, they let out a half-hearted call, and then were utterly shocked when the call was returned by an even louder roaring nearby. At first, they played a game of cat and mouse with the lion around a sandy riverbed thicket, as they walked back and forth, calling in intervals. When the lion roared, Erik tried to move closer to get a better shot; unbeknownst to him, the lion was doing the same thing, walking toward his call to try and pinpoint his location. Eventually, in a lull between the calling, the hunter and Erik carefully crept across a small opening in the sand bed, and then out stepped the lion right in front of them.

When the cat spotted the hunters at less than 100 yards, it stopped and sat down on its haunches with its paws stretched out in front of him and its legs tucked behind- like a clever housecat that has just been caught sneaking around an empty kitchen. The client knelt in similar fashion and slowly aimed his rifle with one elbow resting on his bent knee. Erik had seen the man coolly shoot an eland and buffalo on his short safari so far, and decided to put all his faith in the man now. If he missed or only wounded the lion, they would have little time to finish it off before it charged them.

One well-placed shot through the center of the chest obliterated the lungs and severed the spinal cord on its exit. The magnificent cat collapsed in a heap on the ground. Shortly after this, me and one of the other apprentices named Simon arrived at the scene.

The success of the hunt was exciting, and the lion's very presence there was exhilarating. Still, I couldn't help but feel an equally overwhelming feeling of regret at having cheated in this mortal battle. Seeing such strength and ferocity reduced to a pile of loose flesh by a mechanical weapon felt almost blasphemous. I smiled like a boy as we snapped countless photos of the fallen creature, and I kept my negative thoughts to myself, knowing I was in the company of hunters.

I was surprised when, later in main camp after the client had retired to his bungalow, Erik finally revealed his shared feelings of the day.

"There is perhaps no animal more impressive or beautiful than a living lion," he said with a twinkling smile.

"And equally," he continued, "There is perhaps nothing more depressing or ugly than a dead lion."

The mental strain of hunting lion this way was sometimes too much for our clients. Once, a French PH named Francois took a French client into our northernmost hunting block specifically to hunt lion in the sun-scorched thorn bush where they were more prevalent. It didn't take more than a day to locate a small pride, and after a bait was set up and the animals fed for a few days, the PH decided to build a blind nearby, and then use the metal horn to set up a territorial challenge to the resident male. Despite their often finicky nature, the lion came right into the call. It was so effective, in fact, the hunter had no time to compose himself before the mighty cat appeared in their presence, staring directly at the blind and creeping forward to the sound of the call.

The PH calmly told the man to take the shot. As the lion moved closer, and the seconds ticked by, the PH grew more frantic.

"Shoot, shoot now!" he hissed. And still, nothing came.

Swiveling around, the PH found the old hunter staring wide-eyed at the approaching cat, his face dripping with perspiration and his eyes and mouth open in shock. The man was frozen in terror, unable to even talk or move. After awhile, the clever lion grew nervous, and slowly retreated the way it had come- vanishing in the thorn bush.

When the man did recover from his fright, he tried to save face by swearing he had never seen the lion.

I asked the PH if it were possible the man was telling the truth, and perhaps he hadn't seen the lion. My friend stared at me blankly, and then produced a small digital camera. On the screen, he pulled up a photo of a male lion walking toward the camera at no more than 40 yards.

"I don't know, you tell me," he said with a grin.

Still, out of all of these hunting methods and species, nothing could compare to the thrill and terror of calling in a dominant buffalo bull.

We learned to taunt the buffalo bulls by making a distressed calf call by cupping our mouths and letting out a mournful bellow; this method was so effective, we sometimes even drew the animals in to within an arms' reach. As a hunting technique it was brilliant. Whenever the animals had entered a dense thicket, as they were apt to do, calling them out to get a clear shot was vital. I became quite good at this, even showing off my skills to the legendary PH Mike Fell, by helping draw a buffalo to within shooting range of one of his clients on his very first safari in our area.

It was actually Mike who first pointed out the cattle egrets flying in and out of a seemingly small thicket on the edge of a swampy lake.

"There's buffalo in there, I would bet anything on that!" he said excitedly.

I had not even noticed the birds, let alone considered the fact that they might be following buffalo. But Mike observed how the birds were moving erratically, indicating how the moving buffalo were disturbing them. We positioned ourselves on the edge of the lake and Mike asked me if I knew how to call for the buffalo. I happily obliged, and at my first bellow- a herd of buffalo magically appeared from the thicket, rushing us in an instant.

The client made a good shot with his .416 Rigby, and the encounter lasted little more than a few minutes; easily the fastest- albeit one of the most exciting- buffalo hunts I had ever been a part of.

But I wasn't content calling in the buffalo only on hunting safaris with clients. When egged on by the Africans I worked with in the bush, I began practicing my distress call on buffalo while only lightly armed- and sometimes, not armed at all. God only knows why I did this.

On one foot-expedition deep in the rainforest galleries, me and my two African companions kept encountering one group of buffalo after another. Everywhere we went, we found the bovines- in muddy swamps, wet marshes, forests with tall trees, and grassy plateaus. We competed for who could make the most convincing buffalo calls, and each time the winners were rewarded with an uncomfortably close encounter with the dreaded creatures.

At one point, we repeatedly called into a massive herd of milling cows and calves, hoping to draw out the unseen bull. We got our wish when the herd suddenly parted like the Red Sea and out came the fat patriarch with short stubby horns snorting angrily and thrashing small saplings as he rushed us. We ended up scampering into the nearest trees as the bull ran back and forth below us, bellowing in slobbery rage.

Still, even this encounter didn't compare to what happened the very next time we encountered a herd of buffalo in a patch of long grass in a forest glade.

A group of bachelor bulls were feeding just out of reach of us, led by one bull with especially wide, flat horns. I let out a distressed calf call, and the animals immediately locked in on our position. I stopped calling as the animals approached to within 70 yards or so, milling about trying to find our position. One of the Africans taunted me to call again.

"No," I said, "They are too close."

"Are you scared, *munju?*" he asked, using the derogatory term for white person.

"No," I said, feeling my chest swelling.

"Then prove it, *munju,*" he taunted me with a smile before retreating some distance to await my next move.

With my pride at stake, I let out one weak bellow; but before the call could properly leave my lips, the animals were on us in an instant.

It was the dumbest and most terrifying encounter I had ever had with a buffalo. With only one small sapling separating me from the wide-horned bull, and not enough time or space to retreat, all I could do was curl up and push my head into the dirt with my hands wrapped around the small tree, guarding my head.

Out of my periphery, I could just make out the bull's form looming above me on the other side of the tree, perhaps 3 feet away. The agitated animal began snorting loudly, as drool and snot dangled from his nostrils and mouth. I have never wanted a moment to be over more than I did then, and I tried to will the animal to leave with every wish in my body. Though I didn't consciously make a plea, there were many unspoken requests made to God. I closed my eyes and muttered under my breath, *"fuck, fuck, fuck…"*

It might be cliché to say, but those few seconds lasted hours. A sudden stomping of hooves next to my head made me fear for an instant that I was about to be gored, but it was only the buffalo turning away in retreat. I didn't dare open my eyes and look up for a long moment, until I heard the murderous laughter erupting behind me from my two African companions.

"That was close, eh!?" the instigator said laughing and wagging his finger, as if to scold me.

I stood up slowly, leaning with my hands on my knees, unable to catch my breath.

"No more," was all I could mutter.

The next day, we encountered another herd of buffalo feeding on the edge of a forest salt-lick. My companions looked at me expectedly, but I didn't even smile. There would be no more taunting buffalo for the rest of the expedition. In fact, it would be the last time I would ever intentionally pick a fight with a dangerous African animal again.

Chapter 9: Lost

In April 2009, at the closing of my first safari season in the bush, I was able to lead one last exploratory expedition deep in the southern reaches of our hunting concession. Here, the savanna woodlands of the mighty eland merged into the genuine primary rainforests of the mysterious bongo.

With the first rains of the year, a thin carpet of lush grass covered everything. The trees were sprouting new leaves, giving a vibrant hue to the entire landscape. There was a silence here that was almost unnerving. The soul of the place somehow felt older. The local guys talked about rumors of a cryptic population of chimpanzees hiding out in the farthest reaches of this area. They called the place Tatara. It lay at the confluence of the Tatara and Chinko rivers, in an area especially full of virgin forests and meadows.

For two weeks we had been toiling to cut a new road here- my team of a dozen Africans and myself. I had not spoken English that entire time, and so was forced to learn the local language, Sango more earnestly. Every day we exhausted ourselves clearing this new 4x4 trail with machetes, axes, and shovels. My hands were so blistered and calloused I winced every time I wrapped my palms around my tools. I needed a break from the work.

After we arrived to a flat hilltop above what appeared to have once been an ancient volcano, we decided to set up a long-term base camp. This volcanic plateau was the spot my boss Erik had instructed me to clear a makeshift airstrip for his ultra-light aircraft. We located it on Google Earth satellite images before starting the expedition. Just south of this spot, we also located a likely location of a salt-lick in the forest.

One day after leaving the men to the job of clearing the airstrip runway, I decided to take a leisurely stroll to check out this new salt-lick.

From our makeshift airstrip, the heavily used game trails leading to the salt-lick were almost as defined as a neighborhood sidewalk in suburban America. I decided to leave my big backpack there- not wanting the burden of carrying heavy equipment I wouldn't need. Instead, I brought a small fanny pack with only essential survival gear and my Nikon camera.

The game trails lead from the top of the open plateau down a steep slope toward a dense patch of forest. Within 15 minutes, the open country was gone- taking with it the sound of the cheerful Africans busy at work.

Where the game trails ended, rays of sunlight cut through the rainforest canopy, revealing the salt-lick: a 200 yard wide circular area of mud pocked with animal tracks. A troop of baboons screamed away in retreat as I arrived. In the canopy, Blue Turaco birds- looking like miniature velociraptors- danced across the tree branches, scattering tiny wild figs with their erratic movement. Muddy clouds in the pools of standing water on the salt-lick surface revealed that large animals had just left. A sharp barnyard smell coming from a scattering of cow-pies easily identified the recent visitors as a herd of buffalo.

Damn, I just missed them, I thought.

I walked across the muddy salt-lick examining all the tracks in order to get an idea of what had been visiting the area. Although I saw a few tracks that looked like they could have belonged to bongo, the entire area had been so heavily stampeded by buffalo, I could not confidently identify any species other than the large bovine.

Satisfied with my short exploration of the area, I turned back toward camp. As I climbed the hill, I soon found my previous approach confused by this new perspective: what seemed like one distinct direction of large game trails, now looked like a collection of game trails heading in every direction. Still, the approach from camp was so short and direct- I decided to push straight ahead without much thought

As I scrambled up through the thin clusters of trees along the hillside, something caught my eye: under a pile of low hanging branches lay the bleached white bones of a large animal.

The first bone I could tell was a femur, and I didn't even need to see the skull lying a few yards uphill to know it belonged to an elephant. I squatted there on my heels for a long moment, contemplating the remains. It was a small elephant; out there, in the gauntlet of generations of highly experienced Sudanese ivory poachers- elephants don't grow old. In our main hunting areas within the concession, sightings of elephants- or even their sign- was almost non-existent. But here, in the real forest, a few of them remained.

Just a few days before, one of my African companions and I had been sneaking through the forest calling for duikers, when we suddenly flushed out a small group of elephants at close range. And even in the forests around the airstrip, fresh elephant dung littered the ground of our makeshift campsite. Still, the animals were rare enough in these parts that the elephant bones brought only a somber feeling to my short hike to the salt-lick. I continued walking.

The steep hill above the salt-lick soon flattened into the plateau I had just descended from, but something wasn't right. The area was supposed to be completely open- but in that moment, I was caught in a thick tangle of scrubby bushes. Stubbornly, I pushed forward, driving further and further into the brush. I climbed a small tree to get a better vantage of the area. As far as I could see, the thicket stretched on toward the horizon. I had somehow managed to get myself trapped in a thicket within a few hundred yards of camp.

As the panic began to well inside me, I frantically opened my fanny pack and started searching for my GPS. My heart sank when I realized it was with my backpack... the backpack I had left in camp. Now, the panic I had been suppressing began to grip me. I started clawing my way forward, anxious to get out of the tangled maze. The thorn covered branches of the bushes around me clawed and cut my exposed limbs. I wanted to scream, but I was too exhausted even for this.

When I finally managed to claw my way painfully through the maze of thorn and bramble onto the open grassland- nothing looked familiar. From atop the volcanic plateau where the airstrip was being created, it was easy to make out landmarks, since we were above everything. Now, I was somewhere at mid-level on the plateau, and everything looked the same. Half of my surroundings were composed of dense forests, and the other half was composed of thick woodlands clustered on the open grassland. I decided to continue walking in the open areas and to keep the forests to my left, since I knew crossing even one patch of the rainforest would make me irreversibly lost. Gathering a deep breath, I set off.

Because of the fresh rains, bright flowers were beginning to sprout in the lush green grass that covered the plateau- especially the famed African Blood lily, which exploded in bright reds from the contrasting green. If it wasn't for the worry that loomed over me like a gray cloud, I would have thoroughly enjoyed the sunny stroll. I walked through hundreds of scattered cap-topped termite mounds- which looked like tiny fairy homes and are unique to Central and West Africa (unlike the massive termite mounds found in eastern and southern Africa).

I distinctly remember walking over a fallen log that had been encased in red-termite paste dirt. As my foot landed on the other side, I heard a loud thumping underneath me, like some animal escaping. I ran forward looking back at the log when suddenly- out from an old aardvark hole I had nearly fallen into, came bursting a large Warthog boar. Both the pig and I made a sidestepping jump to avoid colliding into one another.

There we stared at each other for a long moment, my heart racing as large clouds of dust blew off the animal's leathery back. Then, it whirled away and was gone. I had to laugh out loud to calm the fright the unexpected appearance of the creature caused.

After the warthog incident, it didn't take long before the monotony of the same scenery once again lulled me into complacency. I walked past hundreds of termite mounds, sidestepped dozens of fallen logs, pushed through innumerable waste-high scrub brush, and then suddenly- I bumped into a wall of buffalo.

Instinctively, I dropped to a crouch behind a low bush, and my eyes strained forward to assess the scene.

The buffalo apparently hadn't seen me, as they continued feeding obliviously. By now, the Yellow-beaked oxpeckers squawking on the creature's backs were so loud, I cursed myself for not picking up on their presence sooner. Thinking I had gotten away with the blunder, I eased back comfortably, observing the animals. As my eyes traced each of them in number from left to right, with animals ranging from calves, juveniles, mature cows, young bulls, and at least two large bulls- my eyes suddenly froze on one angry cow staring directly at me.

Even the exaggerated furrowed eyebrows of a pissed-off cartoon character couldn't reveal an animal's emotions more distinctly than that face burning a hole in me. The gig was up, and only she and I knew it in that moment. She stepped forward, standing protectively between two calves- one dark brown and one light orange- apparently her babies.

I held my breath in the strain of that awful moment, hoping she wouldn't draw the herd's attention to me. And then she stomped and snorted frantically. Every animal lifted its head and stared directly at me as I cowered behind a frail little bush.

After a long moment, every animal turned to my left and began stampeding away. One old bull paused for a moment to look at me, and I snapped a photo of it- a picture which now makes up the cover of this book. After the stampede, only the angry cow remained. She stayed there, scowling at me with her head held low, menacingly. Only after the last calf had departed in a cloud of dust, did the cow turn to follow them. Tossing her head up, she gave me one last disdainful snort before disappearing.

My knees were shaking from adrenaline as they went, but a new fear replaced them when I noticed the sun was eerily low against the trees. It would be dark soon, and I was not prepared for another night alone in the bush.

Earlier that season, my GPS had malfunctioned under dense rainforest canopy on another solo salt-lick reconnaissance, and by the time I emerged onto the savanna, the sun was setting, and I was too far from camp to risk a night march. So, I was forced to hunker where I was, quickly building a massive fire for company. The spot was incidentally only a few miles away from where I had bumped into a sleeping lion in the long grass a few days before. Needless to say, I slept poorly that night.

Now, lost on top of the volcanic plateau, I was dreading the thought of spending another night alone in the bush. By now, I was also terribly thirsty, and I began contemplating going down into the rainforest to get water. I knew there was water to be found in the trees- but I had no idea how far until I would reach it: a few hundred yards? A few miles? I also had nothing to carry the water to continue my walk, since I had left my bottle with my gear. I began picking up large, dried, hollowed-out Monkey fruit shells that lay scattered across the plateau.

These, I could use as water gourds if I absolutely needed to. By popping the top stem off, I could collect perhaps a cup's worth of water in each one. I took off my undershirt and gathered these inside, before tying the entire bundle over my shoulder like a book-bag.

I continued to walk, keeping the forest to my left the entire time. I knew, whatever I was going to do, I had to keep the forest to my left. But the thought of entering it for the night began to entice me.

Just as the sun was beginning to set, I heard the sharp pang of a machete. Running to the sound, I began hearing voices. Coming over a cliff overhang, I could barely make out the men below me, 500 yards away, finishing their work on the airstrip and preparing for the night. I hustled as fast as I could to reach them, for darkness was now moments away.

As I neared the group of cheerful men, I intentionally slowed my walk and put on a cool, calm demeanor.

"Adam!" one of my companions, Yaya, shouted in greeting. "Did you get lost?" he asked in half-amused worry.

By now, everyone was quiet, staring intently at me, waiting for my answer.

"Of course not," I said confidently. "I just went for a little walk."

Chapter 10: Cryptids of the African Bush

When traveling the far corners of Sub-Saharan Africa, where lonely communities live on the fringes of primordial wilderness, one inevitably comes across strange tales of mysterious creatures. Often, these tales border between superstitious fantasy and the realm of possibility. In the unexplored eastern corner of the Central African Republic- some of these tales turned out to be genuine; And others remain a mystery yet to be proven.

The first and most compelling cryptid tale I heard, was of a mysterious saber-toothed cat, called a *Ruju*, that supposedly had non-retractable claws (like a cheetah), and a hunched back like a hyena- with a short, stubby tale. This cat was said to have lived in swamps of the deep forested regions south of the Mbari and Chinko rivers, and hunted forest pigs as its primary prey.

I first heard about the animal while sitting around a campfire in the bush with my boss, Erik Mararv, and a group of local poachers. A prolific poacher named Mohomet, who had earned a reputation in the area as one of the best elephant hunters, lead the conversation. With animated displays with erratic, outstretched arms, he described coming upon a scene of a Ruju attack, where the saber-toothed cat had ambushed a group of Red River hogs walking through a muddy trench in a rainforest swamp. He described the animal as having waited for the hogs to walk below him and then jumping on the back of one, sinking its dagger-length canine teeth into its neck and spine.

A few other hunters in the circle around our campfire took turns sharing their similar encounters with the saber-toothed cat during their excursions in the bush. Two brothers, Hassan and Issan, described how they had inadvertently caught one of the creatures in a snare they had set for antelope. Upon approaching the animal, it sprang at them in a charge, ripping free from the snare and coming at them full bore. They had to carefully aim their single-shot shotguns and fire in quick succession at the animal's chest to kill it.

My Sango at that time (this was my first season in CAR) was very poor, and I struggled to follow the exact details of these stories, although I could make out the main points. Erik filled me in on the parts I missed.

I was surprised how calm and expressionless Erik looked as he listened to such fantastical tales. And so, I asked him afterwards, "Do you believe in the stories of this saber-toothed cat?"

"Do I believe some saber-toothed cat- remnants of the Ice Age- somehow survived for thousands of years, isolated in a small pocket in the heart of Central Africa?" Erik responded rhetorically. "Not likely. But it doesn't matter what I think. To these men, this animal does exist in their world."

When we inquired if there was evidence in the shape of a skull or skin to confirm the stories of the animal, they said they had not saved any. They went on to say that the Ruju was only encountered very rarely- and almost never taken by a hunter's bullet. Erik and I both promised the men a large prize purse of money if they could successfully bring back the skin and skull of such an animal. This excited the group of men immediately, and they quickly promised to fulfill this within a year or two. Alas, for the next five years while I was there, no evidence for such an animal was ever produced.

Another animal the men talked about was the *Yogu*, which they described as "a small duiker- the size of a blue duiker- with stripes" that supposedly lived deep in the mangrove-like forests on the edge of rivers like the Mbari.

In our area, we knew we had over a half-a-dozen duiker species, ranging from the 4lb blue duiker, to the 120lb Yellow-backed duiker. However, none of these animals had stripes. In the minds of the Professional Hunters in the company, the only animal we could imagine from these tales, were the Zebra duikers found in the dense forests of West Africa; an antelope looking almost exactly like a blue duiker, but with whitish-gray fur, and black stripes down its flanks. To us, the persistent rumors from the local poachers had to indicate that somehow, a population of this animal had to exist in the Chinko basin, separated for thousands of miles from its only known population to the west.

Ever so often, while sleeping out in the bush near the Mbari, the men would alert me to the sound of a chirping noise near the water's edge, and excitedly told me it was made by the Yogu. Hurriedly, we would fetch our flashlights and set off in pursuit, fighting through the tangled foliage, hoping to get a glimpse of the creature making the sound. But always, our searches turned out fruitless.

Finally, in 2011, the mystery of the Yogu was revealed while I drove down the road toward the nearest village, Bakouma, situated along the thick forest regions where the Yogu were said to exist. Coming upon a group of local meat poachers walking barefoot with their night's catch hanging limp on their shoulders, we asked the men what they had killed: I noticed right away the Colobus monkey, African Putty-nosed monkey, blue duiker- and then, a strange animal I had never seen up close before- the African Water chevrotain.

The chevrotain is an ancient species of animal that predates modern antelope and is found throughout Asia as well, where it is referred to as the "mouse deer." The animal's fur has splotches of both white stripes and white spots spattered across its rusty reddish-brown fur. They also have tiny, curved fangs in their mouths- like many early deer and antelope species. Remarkably, they can swim under water for long periods of time- a skill they often use to evade predators. I had only ever glimpsed one in the wild, when I disturbed it near a rainforest creek, and watched it belly flop in the water, before completely submerging itself and swimming away- with only tiny air bubbles indicating its route of escape.

As I inspected the animal closely, one of the men on the back of the truck congratulated me excitedly on my good fortune, for this was indeed the Yogu. As it turned out, our "striped duiker" wasn't a cryptid after-all.

Early on in our development of the Chinko and Mbari basins- we heard rumors of chimpanzees existing in the forest regions especially in the south-east of our concessions. Only one westerner, a French Professional Hunter working on the south-eastern side of Chinko, ever reported finding evidence of the animals in the form of nests. Apart from this, there was little evidence to substantiate these rumors.

But the big blank spot on the map of the deep forested area taunted my imagination. The fact that no formal study had ever been conducted in hundreds upon hundreds of miles of the secretive rainforests further excited my imagination. I decided early on that chimpanzees had to be there- not because I had evidence, but because my fantasies wanted to will it into reality.

When two researchers named Theirry and Rafael arrived to the hunting concession in 2012 to conduct the first wildlife survey of the area, they came with rather low expectations in what cryptid animals they might find there. They believed that populations of African wild dogs- a species critically endangered in most of their ranges outside of national parks- existed in the wilderness of the eastern Central African Republic. I was one of the first to greet them in the bush, as they drove through the Mbari forest camp on their way to Kocho camp.

When we met, they excitedly asked me if I had by chance seen any wild dogs. I responded by pulling up a collection of photos of wild dogs I had taken over the last few years, and descriptions of where exactly I had found them. The two men nearly fell over in their chairs. Back in Europe, their colleagues and other "wildlife experts" swore the animals did not exist here.

The first time I saw the animals was during a long expedition to the Tatara region my first year as an apprentice. I saw a pair of the canines running around, nipping at each other and tussling around playfully like domestic dogs. From then on, the creatures began turning up everywhere around our concession, with the largest pack- at least 30 animals- hanging out around our main Kocho camp. They would often chase our cars late at night, nipping at our tires. And their presence prompted me to carry a machete on my morning jogs just outside of camp: I reasoned that, like most dogs, an aggressive African wild dog might find a wop on the nose of the flattened end of my blade to be a deterrent. I'm still grateful I never had to test this theory.

In 2014, while taking a lunch break with my African trackers after scouting a new area, I decided to sit down in the shade of a small forest next to some termite mounds- and immediately the small forest erupted in bellowing barks that sent me and my companions running to the car for my rifle. As it turned out, we had inadvertently stumbled on a wild dog den site. Excitedly, I gathered some fresh droppings from the site and took them back to Theirry and Rafael to be studied. They quickly returned to the site and set up some inferred camera traps.

The photos of the tiny African wild dogs emerging from their burrows is a gift I cherish to this day, and an exciting reminder of our "discovery" of an important population of animals once thought to be extinct in those parts.

But the surprising discoveries did not end here.

A year after I left Africa, the two researchers carried out an even larger survey of the area, in which they physically transected the unexplored forest region. Here, they observed in the flesh, a group of chimpanzees, perhaps the northern-most population ever to be discovered in Africa! Further surveys revealed the population to be in the multi-hundreds, suggesting it could be one of the largest and most important large primate populations discovered in recent memory.

There are some animal mysteries in the Chinko basin that will forever taunt my imagination as long as their presence remains unproven.

First, early on in the development of the northern Chinko hunting concessions, two different road cutting crews swore to have spotted cheetah. In the northern plains of the headwaters of the Chinko, this would have been suitable habitat for the animals. The eyewitnesses were also reliable- so I have no reason to doubt them. The only thought that haunts me, is the fact that cheetah, if they still existed in the region in the 2010s, would have already been small in number: and after the Mbororo cow herdsmen invaded the area around that same time- specifically choosing the grazing areas well-suited for cheetah- it is unlikely they could have shared the same habitat for long before the herdsman would have killed them.

Another animal that has always existed in the psyche of the local hunters I shared hundreds of nights around the campfire with, is the forest sitatunga: a medium sized, dark gray antelope with white stripes and spiral horns that lives a semi-aquatic lifestyle in the swamps and marshes in the rainforests of Central Africa.

I have no doubt the animals exist here, as I have heard countless stories of them from my ex-poacher friends who have no reason to lie about an animal they describe as readily as a bongo or buffalo- animals known to exist in large numbers in the region. However, for whatever reason, no Professional Hunter or wildlife researcher working in the area has ever proven their existence in the form of camera trap or reliable sighting. On my Tatara expedition, in a vast marshland surrounded by dense forests, I did find what I believe to be the tracks of sitatunga- with their distinctive splayed step. I suspect the animals exist in small, isolated populations, and their secretive habits and even more secretive choice of habitats, is the reason they have remained unseen by Western eyes.

Another time, I had a brief encounter with a mysterious animal whose identity has confounded me for years. While walking through a narrow forest gallery in northern Chinko, I caught sight of a tiny monkey scurrying through some tree branches just above me. That it was a monkey and not a galago was unmistakable- although it was small like a bush baby. It had a round face with big monkey ears and eyes, long, sinewy limbs, and a thin, curling monkey tail. It was incredibly small- much smaller than any known monkey species in the area. The only creature that resembles the animal I saw, is a Talapoin; a tiny monkey found thousands of miles away and restricted to the western coast of Africa.

What set this sighting apart, was that I actually snapped some photos of the creature; or rather, poor glimpses of the animal's arms, legs, and tail as it departed. But even with these cryptic photos of only small parts of the animal, one immediately notices they differ from any known monkey in the region. Even years later, wildlife researchers reached out to examine the photos themselves. To this day, as far as I know, no one has been able to identify this mystery monkey species- which begs the question: what other unknowns does this wild region of Africa hold?

I for one hope some of these wild mysteries remain unanswered. For as long as men have marched through the desolate places of the world and sailed its seas- myths of unknown monsters have prowled the periphery of their consciousness, making the adventures that much grander. One can plainly see this inscribed on the ancient explorers' maps that show sketches of dragons, sea monsters and other beasts; or in cruder paintings surviving on cave walls. For it is the mystery of the unknown that makes the darkness around the campfire much larger and more intriguing. As long as there are still unanswered mysteries out there in the wild places of the world, there are reasons to venture out and explore them.

The author during his first-year apprenticeship, pausing on a hill during a multi-day exploratory trek to investigate bongo salt-licks along the Mbari river forests

The mighty Chinko river

Lead tracker Charles stands next to a tree encased by a large termite mound

The author admiring a mature Lord Derby's eland bull. This was the first eland hunt he guided as a Professional Hunter

Building a high-stand overlooking a bongo salt-lick deep in the forest. Such work was treacherous

The author investigating a cave in the forest

A magnificent Lord Derby's eland bull, taken by the author's client not far from the Chinko river. This bull measured well over 50-inches

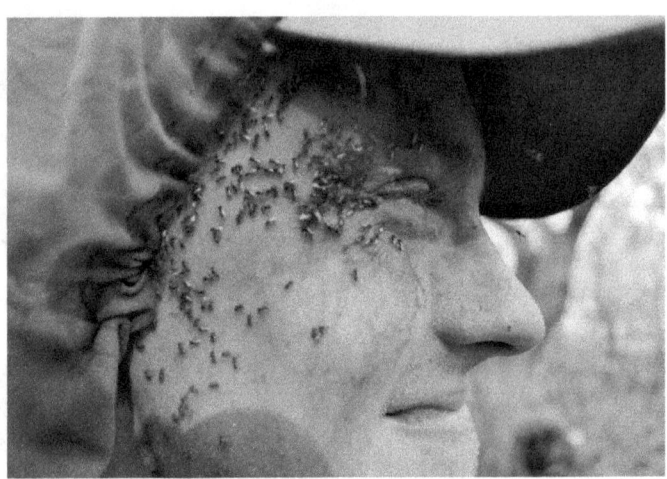

Mopani flies were a constant annoyance in the Guinean savanna woodlands

Charles (left) and Gambou (right) carry a good bushbuck male out of a clearing in the rainforest

A savanna buffalo bull feeding in a forest opening near the Chinko river at dusk

The author with a Nile crocodile he captured by hand and later released along the Mbari river

A group of local workers and trackers piled on their Toyota Land Cruiser during a road cutting expedition

The author with a good Roan bull

African rock python

Giant forest hog boar on a salt-lick near the Chinko river

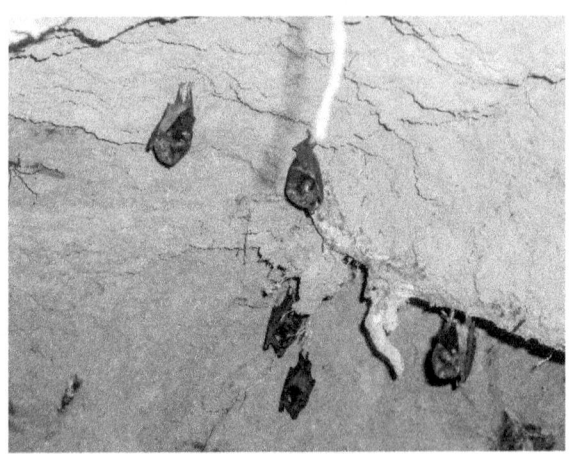

Small bats hanging on the roof of a cave in the forest

The author with an ancient bongo bull taken by an American client near the Mbari river

Local worker scanning an open plateau along the Chinko river

Crossing the Mbari river during high water was a treacherous endeavor on our small ferry

The author with a bushbuck. One of the few personal trophies he took during his time in the bush

A western Kob male photographed not far from the Chinko river

The author standing in a salt-lick overhang dug out of a hillside by generations of elephants. The marks of both elephant tusks and eland horns can be seen etched into the clay

(From left to right) Allen, Charles, Gambou, and the author pose behind a big Red River hog boar taken in a thick riverine forest

Gambou lashes the feet of a Red River hog with tree vines before carrying it out of the forest

The author poses behind a Yellow-backed duiker male he personally took during a road cutting expedition

Gambou (center) walks with two local hunters during a multi-day trek into bongo country

Traditional dance carried out by locals in the Kocho main camp to celebrate a successful lion hunt

A local man poses with the discarded sheaths of a buffalo killed by lions on a salt-lick, found during a trek into bongo country

A Lelwel hartebeest male photographed not far from the Chinko river

The author poses behind an exceptional Giant Forest hog boar, taken on a salt-lick by an American hunter near the Ngoy river

A rare photo of a Lord Derby's eland bull taken in the open with his harem, photographed near the Kocho river. This photo, taken by the author, has been widely shared

An impressive Lord Derby's eland bull with the author's .458 Lott

The thick tuft of hair on a mature Giant eland bull's face, characteristic of the sub-species

The tracks of a mature bongo antelope on a forest salt-lick

Erik Mararv celebrating a sucessful hunt in main camp

Bienvenue, the legendary ex-elephant poacher turned conservation ranger.

The author with an impressive savanna buffalo bull he put down at close range during a follow up

Opening the safari roads after a long rainy season when the grass grew as tall as a person

The author with the bold leopard described in Chapter 1

The author poses with a mature lion during his first-year apprenticeship, taken by a European client. Male lions in the Central African Republic often do not grow the large manes characteristic of populations found in eastern and southern Africa

(From left to right) Charles, Allen, and the author resting in their makeshift campsite during an exploratory trek in the southern Chinko region. The team would encounter elephants during this trip

A mature Warthog boar

A venomous Puff adder well-hidden in the leafy forest floor

Two trackers carrying a bongo cape out of the forest

A Red-flanked duiker standing in a Guinea savanna woodland

Mattheo inspects a fresh harvest of honey taken at night during a road-cutting expedition

A herd of bongo antelope led by an impressive bull, standing in a forest salt-lick

The author standing in front of a salt-lick cave, carved out of a hillside by generations of elephants. Sadly, few elephants survive in the Chinko basin after decades of relentless poaching by heavily armed North Sudanese poachers

A large rock python devouring a female bushbuck in a forest stream

The author standing behind a mature savanna buffalo bull

Professional Hunter Anton using a horn to call for lions - a technique unique to the Central African Republic

The author taking a lunch break during a multi-day exploratory trek in the forest regions

Scenes from main camp: (left) A guest house

Dining area along the Kocho river

Dining area with bar

Garage with fleet of work vehicles

Kocho main camp staff posing in the kitchen area

A family of Black-and-white colobus monkeys lived in the canopy above Kocho main camp

(From left to right) Allen, the author, Gambou, and Charles pose behind a bongo antelope bull, taken during the author's last season working as a Professional Hunter

Chapter 11: *Bozobo*, Lord of the Savanna

The Lord Derby's eland is the royal king of the ungulate world. He is big and formidable, graceful and elusive, with large piercing eyes that give no other accurate description than intelligence. His neck, during the rut, is too thick for the largest man to wrap his arms around. Grizzled hair runs from his forehead down to his spinal blade; draped like a coal black cape, hanging on a dewlap of loose skin on his throat. There is no other comparison in the antelope world.

I have seen tough men cry, after days and days of toil, studying every step of the prey under the intense African sun, finally gracing their hands over their grand, Lord Derby's eland. It has taken me a handful of years guiding hunts for these wondrous creatures, with men of all shapes and sizes, to fully appreciate that this is indeed one of the most difficult and rewarding hunts in the world.

Surely, the bushmen and early Stone-Age people already knew this, when trying to close the gap to within spear or bow range of the wary animals. It must have felt eternally impossible, even for their superior hunting skills, to touch the lords of the savanna woodland; except for the odd chance encounter, when the stars aligned and they found it possible. Today, with our scoped rifles, we have only just now evened the odds somewhat to match the incredible eyesight, hearing and smell of these creatures.

The hunt for the Lord Derby's eland in the far reaches of Cameroon and the Central African Republic has changed little, if at all, from what early 20th century African safaris used to be. To bag the royal king of antelopes, the keen hunter best lace up their boots, pack their bag full of food and water, and strike out into the Sub-Saharan bush on foot.

For a solid week in January 2014 in the eastern CAR, my friend and client Henrik and I had not so much as even seen a fresh eland track. When we finally found the track of an old solitary bull one morning on a salt-lick from the night before, it was with high anticipation we followed it. We were hoping to catch the bull in his midday resting place. For six hours that eland led us on a wild ride through flat grassland, and thick Mopani woodland, through a dense forest, and finally into the long dry grass of a high plateau. The sign was fresh, but the bull always stayed just out of reach. When he led us through the long grass, we knew the day's hunt was over. We could not track as fast as he was walking. We reluctantly left the track and made it back to the car at dusk.

Hunters are strange people, and usually gluttons for punishment. When we found the same bull's tracks, huge and enticing on the same salt lick a few days later, we couldn't resist but follow again. The bull was kinder to us this day, and took us on a gentler course, through shady woods and into a cool forest after an easy three hours. But an "easy" eland day is as difficult as the hardest of hunting days anywhere else, and we sat down in the forest to catch our breath and nourish ourselves with food and water. After maybe an hour, a whistle roused me from a daydream, and I found my three trackers Gambou,

Samson, and Allen squatting in front of me, eager to get on the track again. They had found the eland's trail on the other side of the forest, in an area with better soil for tracking. The enthusiasm was contagious, and we followed the bull with renewed encouragement.

Imagine our surprise when, after an hour or so more, we found our "solitary" bull track suddenly turn into a mess of tracks, from many different animals, ranging from babies to mature animals. The bull had integrated into a herd in the late morning, and we were right behind them. For this period of early January, right before the rut, often these solitary bulls will enter and exit a herd, waiting for the cows to come into heat. Eland are not as aggressive as many other species of mammal, and multiple bulls in a single herd will tolerate each other.

We were all exhausted from the endless hours of strained attention to the track, and were starting to let our guard down. At around 5:15pm- just thirty minutes before dark, we looked up, and there, 50 yards in front of us, was the herd of eland. Miraculously, they were feeding and blissfully unaware of us!

Henrick and I crept forward behind a clump of trees, leaving the trackers behind. There were perhaps eight animals in close proximity to us. None were shooters, but there were plenty of animals in the back we could not see. After ten minutes or so, with anticipation mounting, we suddenly felt the cool evening wind shift and hit the back of our neck. And just like that, in a cloud of dust, our eight hours of hard work tracking were ruined in a split second. Darkness came, and we walked the two miles back to the truck defeated.

Henrick knew the tracking game well after undertaking many elephant hunts, and when we decided to pick up the tracks where we left off the next day, he wasn't at all discouraged. Under normal conditions, if you physically see eland one day, unless they don't leave the area of hunting roads, you will almost always find them again the very next morning. This was not the case for us. The animals had entered the most rocky, mountainous region in the area. Despite the superior hunting skills of our trackers, we simply could not keep a fresh track long enough to have a chance of catching up to the animals.

Hunting in the Central African Republic can be full of surprises, as we soon found out. Frustrated, we left the eland herd in the mountains, and headed back to the truck, four miles way. We were all distraught and in bad spirits- especially me. I was ahead of the group, pausing to let them catch up, when I looked up and I saw a different group of eland approaching! Once again, we sat on the ground, examining the ten or so animals that came feeding toward us. Now, here was the moment that defined Henrick as an exceptional hunter. There was a bull just 20 yards ahead of us, feeding and unaware of our presence. He was not an old bull, but still a fairly big one. I told Henrick he could shoot the bull. Henrick looked at the animal and then noted aloud that the bull did not have the luxurious black coat that the older bulls carried. I agreed with him. With no further thought or regret, Henrick politely turned down the offer. He was firmly set on only harvesting an old bull, even with only two days left of hunting!

After some time, the animals came forward, and then a female got too close and spooked the entire herd. Like that, they were gone. We headed home, but this time exhilarated by the close sighing. More importantly, Henrick had earned the satisfaction that he could have justifiably taken a Lord Derby's eland bull, but it was not the trophy he was searching for. He would rather go home empty-handed than take an animal he wasn't completely satisfied with. I had immense respect for the man after that.

As an intermission to the eland hunting, we had a rare opportunity to hunt a very large solitary buffalo one evening. These animals, called savanna buffalo, bring the best qualities of typical Cape buffalo features with Dwarf Forest buffalo; this means some are red, some are black; some have wide horns, others have short ones. This particular bull was a rusty gray/red with large horns. We spotted him just before dark, on the edge of the forest. Henrick put a bullet from his .458 Lott square in his shoulder 50 yards away, broadside. We were confident in the shot, and the good amount of blood, but as it was dark we decided to leave the follow-up till the morning.

The follow-up turned into a tense morning, when we found the blood trail had ended after 300 yards. We had a wounded buffalo on our hands in the thickest bush imaginable. It was the worst-case scenario. It took us an hour to walk 300 more yards. The tension ended in a split second when we saw the bull rise from his bed before he could spot us. With a snap-shot the bull was down, and we all breathed a sigh of relief. Henrick's first bullet had somehow not penetrated all the way through the thick skin and muscle, and just barely touched the bull's lung. The wound was enough to kill the animal, though not out-right.

We did get on to another herd of eland the second to last day of the hunt. We were so close to the animals that we had the satisfaction of following a line of soft, green droppings almost the entire day, from early morning to late afternoon. But strange things often happen in the African bush. When we were certain we would soon come upon the resting animals, a thundering, swooshing sound roared above us, as a military helicopter suddenly came into view!

The helicopter was from the Ugandan military. They were flying through our area to resupply troops they had stationed a few hundred miles away, in the town of Obo. They were staging operations to look for the infamous rebel group, the Lord's Resistance Army, who had a last strong hold on the border of South Sudan. Out of all the possible scenarios that could take place in the bush, on this random day, when we were finally close to the animals of our quest- a helicopter rolled in and ruined everything!

After the helicopter incident, the eland were understandably very wary. We followed them till dark, where the tracks led to a wall of tall grass. We looked in disappointment as we found the warm beds of the creatures where they had been mere moments before we arrived. They had laid down next to a patch of burning long grass, and waited until the fires had died down in the evening, and then crossed the small blaze into the tall grass and out of our grasp. We began the long trek back to the car for two hours in the darkness, never again able to catch up to eland the rest of the safari.

Thoroughly disheartened, I retired to the dining area the last night where I joined Henrik for some beer-drinking consolation. Alone next to a fire pit, while other hunters happily reveled in their success, Henrik and I talked quietly about the last few days. The beer working magic on our exhausted thoughts, we began to talk in sentimental tones. The hunting had been hard, but grand. We had pursued the magical animal as persistently as any person could in two weeks- and it still wasn't enough.

In a lingering moment of silence, a smile stretched across Henrik's face, and his eyes began to glisten. The whole two weeks of our journey flashed across his mind, and I saw, clearly, he was content. With or without a trophy to hang on the wall.

"Sometimes," he said looking up at the ceiling to gather his thoughts, and then straight into my eyes, "It's those hunts you are least successful, that you remember the most."

A true hunter if I ever met one: Henrik left the next day with no trophy eland, but with the promise to return next season to pick up where we left off.

The irony of fate revealed itself my very next safari, when my client, a man new to eland hunting, secured a massive trophy the very first day of his safari. Sweating next to the downed bull, after a seven-hour tracking job, the man stated in bewilderment, "Well, if this is how eland hunting typically is, I'm not sure I wouldn't have called it quits after day one."

…And so it goes, in Central Africa, in pursuit of the Holy Grail: the Lord Derby's eland.

Chapter 12 Prince of Disaster

Professional Hunters don't often talk about how absurdly bad some of their clients can be. And I don't blame them: in a profession supported by this wealthy clientele- it isn't in one's best interests to complain about where the money comes from. However, I am no longer a Professional Hunter and have no real desire to ever work as one again, so I have no problem spilling the unpleasant beans.

When I say many of the clients are "bad," I'm not simply talking about their skills as hunters- I am talking about the very characters of these people.

Take, for example, the decrepit former president of a prominent American hunting club who treated the safari staff like slaves his entire stay; even angrily using his fat belly to shove myself and other guests off the foot path whenever he happened to walk past us. Or the enormous, bald European man who incessantly bragged about his sexual exploits with underaged prostitutes in Third-world countries. And I can't forget about the wealthy American who paid some French PHs leasing our area to hunt and kill his animals for him: only leaving his comfortable bed in camp to drive out and pose for a photograph with his "trophy." As it turns out, this particular man had dozens of high-ranking entries in a very prominent hunting record book.

Now, a decade after these experiences, I can finally remove myself from the emotions of such encounters and appreciate the humorous memories these ridiculous people have left on me. Perhaps none of these blundering misadventures stand out more to me than my safari with a man I'll call, the "Prince of Disaster."

There's a reason for the nickname. Before arriving on his hunt, I was told the man was a royal prince of an old Eastern European family (which I won't name). I met my would-be client at the airstrip one winter day in 2012. He was in his 60s, maybe early 70s, and he had a female companion with him who was in her 30s. This was not wholly unusual, as many of these wealthy men traveled with an entourage of young, attractive women. But almost immediately I could tell this particular woman did not fit the stereotype of these young mistresses. She let it be known upon her arrival that she was just a family friend of the client's and would not be treated as his "girlfriend." At this announcement, a sad, almost resolute brooding came over the man, and it stuck with him the entire hunt. Incidentally, the young woman- closer to my own age- began to turn a flirtatious eye toward me, which only made the old hunter's mood even darker.

Well, this is going to be awkward, I thought.

As was our habit with newly arrived hunters, we walked to the edge of our dusty bush airstrip to sight in the rifles in our makeshift shooting range set up between a stand of skeletal Mopani trees on the edge of a rocky hillside. The hunter excitedly pulled out his rifle, a German Blaser R8 in .375 Holland and Holland, with a custom wood stock he had specially designed by a local gunsmith. The most intriguing feature of this stock, was a thumb hole drilled through the grip, leaving only two, thin delicate pieces of wood to hold the bulk of the butt-stock to the frame.

The man proudly handed it to me, and I examined it carefully.

"You don't look impressed," he said, disappointed by my apparent reservations at the design.

"It's beautiful, no doubt about that," I said. "But with such a large caliber, I'm worried about how this thin wood at the grip will hold up to the recoil."

"Ha!" the man snorted. "An expert gunsmith milled this. I'll put my money on his work."

And put his money on it he did.

When we arrived to our main hunting camp along a picturesque Kocho river later that afternoon, the hunter excitedly showed his prized rifle to my boss, Erik Mararv, who took one look at it, and remarked dryly, "This thumb hole design might be problematic with such a large recoil."

The next day, while quietly walking a dark forest edge shrouded in morning fog, we chanced upon a beautiful Yellow-backed duiker male- an exceptionally elusive rainforest antelope. I threw up my shooting sticks for the hunter to rest his rifle on, and then moved to the side to cover my ears in anticipation of the rifle's boom. When it came, the duiker dropped, stone dead. Smiling, I began slapping the client on his back in congratulations, only to find the man cursing profusely. There, in each hand, he held the severed ends of his beloved rifle where it had snapped in half at the thin thumb hole at the butt grip.

I did not risk saying a word to the angry hunter, as we drove in silence the entire way back to Kocho. There, we picked up our spare .375 H&H CZ camp gun- a humble, beat-up old workhorse of a rifle- for the client to use the remainder of the safari.

The Prince was targeting two specific species on his safari: Leopard and bongo.

So, every afternoon we would make our way to one of the many bongo salt-licks we had staked out deep in the rainforests, and stay for the night, hunting well into the morning. Then, during the heat of the day, we drove around checking leopard baits we had hung in the area. This meant shooting a couple baboons and warthogs to keep as a fresh supply of bait.

We drove a circuit every day checking each of the four baits. For the first three days, there was nothing. And then on the fourth day we got a lucky break.

One of our bait sites was located in a tree with an idyllic overhanging branch nestled against a wall of forest. This branch, where the warthog meat was hung, stretched out over a carpet of long green grass. The approach to this tree was 100 yards or more through a tangle of thick green foliage. We weren't too quiet on our approach, as it was midday and we weren't expecting to see any animals during these hot hours. When I reached the base of the tree, I was startled to find myself staring directly into the curling tail of a leopard, which lay resting on the large overhanging branch nearly eye-level with me.

About the moment I blundered into the cat, the cat saw me, and its fumbling retreat told me it had been equally caught off guard by my appearance. The Prince was just behind me in time to see the blur of spots bounding away into the forest. We decided immediately to stake our place in the leafy blind we had built a few days before, and await the leopard's inevitable return.

I knew the cat would return sooner or later to check on its meal, and I didn't want to be caught by it as we were sneaking into the blind, so we hurried inside. I gave some last-minute instructions to my trackers, and then had them seal off our door into the blind. From there, we waited quietly inside.

The hunter was diligent about keeping quiet and still when we first entered the blind. But like an impatient child, he quickly began to grow restless. First, it started with him frantically swatting the buzzing flies around his face, shaking the edges of the blind with his errant elbows. Then, he began to scratch his arms and legs, as if some phantom crawling insects were infiltrating his pant and arm sleeves.

I looked over at the man until we made eye contact, and whispered to him to keep still. After this brief lull in my concentration, I glanced back up into the tree and found the leopard resting full body across the large overhanging branch, staring directly at us. I had not heard even the wind from the animal's approach.

I grabbed the client's leg tightly, and pointed into the tree, while pressing my finger to my lips. "Shhh," I hissed.

The man stared up into the tree with a blank, bewildered expression on his face. The leopard was less than 40 yards away from us, stretched out in full view; its bright yellow and black fur standing starkly contrasted from the green background. I studied the leopard carefully, trying to determine its sex. After a few minutes of this, I was startled by a loud noise to my left. I turned to find the client struggling to remove his shoes, cursing at some ants that had crawled inside.

At this, the leopard threw itself out of the tree and disappeared.

I grabbed the man's arm tightly and whispered, "You just scared the leopard out of the tree, did you not see it?"

But the man only looked at me annoyed, and clearly did not believe me. It was incomprehensible to me that the man could have missed seeing the cat while it was stretched out in full view in front of us. Gruffly, I instructed the man to stop moving, lest he ruin the hunt.

An hour later, the leopard returned. This time, it was onto our game. The cat climbed the tree but kept its body concealed at the crook, and pulled the bait with its claws down so it could eat in privacy. Again, the animal's face was in plain view, loudly tearing chunks out of the meat and gnashing it up with its teeth. But just to be sure the client wouldn't miss the leopard again, I grabbed his arm tightly and pointed into the tree excitedly.

By now, I decided to pull out my small camera and film the cat as it fed.

As I was fixated on this, I was suddenly startled once again by a loud noise to my left, and found the hunter pushing a section of the leafy blind away from his body, loudly rearranging leaves and branches. I was completely aghast- not only because he was making such a loud noise in front of the leopard, but that he was somehow oblivious to the very presence of the cat.

By now, the leopard was completely fed up, and began growling loudly from its place in the crook of the tree, like a diesel engine revving up in the cold. *GRRR!*

This finally got the hunter's attention, and he suddenly turned to me excitedly pointing in the direction of the growling leopard. But before anything could be done, the leopard whirled away into the forest, grunting loudly as it went. Soon, the bush was quiet once again.

With only 30 minutes left of daylight, and knowing our chances of the leopard returning for us to get a shot was slim to none, I abandoned our hunt for the day. As I began packing everything up to leave, the client became confrontational.

"Why are we leaving so early, there is still daylight left, and the leopard has just returned to the bait!" he protested.

When I informed the man that the leopard had stood in front of us twice now for a full 20 minutes or more, the man flat-out refused to believe it. When I pulled up the camera and showed the man the footage of the leopard feeding, he still did not believe it had been filmed that very moment. And so, I had to show him the time-stamp on the video to prove it. Incredibly, for the rest of the night the man blamed me for his failed leopard hunt.

Our bongo hunting endeavors did not fair much better.

Early in the hunt, we were gifted with a beautiful, solitary male bongo standing straight in the middle of our main forest salt-lick one evening. This particular animal stood about 150 yards away, in a clearing the size of a football field, carelessly nuzzling the ground broadside to us. The hunter took his time aiming, and carefully pulled the trigger.

But nothing happened at the shot. The bongo looked up, startled and confused, and then took off in a slow trot, running directly at our high-stand, confused. At 70 yards or so, the hunter fired again. And still, nothing happened. The animal soon disappeared into the forest, and we saw nothing else the rest of that night or the next morning.

As we left the high-stand, the hunter angrily insisted that the old camp rifle was to blame for the failure. He had been constantly criticizing the beat-up old rifle since he was forced to use it after his ridiculously designed personal rifle had broken. The man, accustomed to only hunting with $30,000+ custom engraved rifles- held the camp rifle with obvious disgust every time it was in his hands.

Not wanting to argue with the man, I decided to humor him, and we promptly went to test fire the rifle once again. And not surprisingly, the rifle was deadly accurate at 100 yards.

After two frustrating weeks of hunting under these conditions, the safari finally neared its conclusion. All that was left to do was to leave our forest camp and drive the last few hours to main camp, where a charter plane would take the hunter away the next morning. As we were packing up our things in camp, the client decided to leave the obligatory tip of cash to the safari employees. For me, the sum he left was abysmal- but I fully expected this, since he had not killed either a leopard or bongo, and was clearly not satisfied with the results. However, it was the even lowlier tip he left for the African trackers and camp staff that really annoyed me.

Even as the hunter was thoroughly disheartened and frustrated by the hunt, I decided to approach him with an idea to sit over one last salt-lick for his final evening on our way back to main camp, in the hopes that we might get a Hail Mary shot at a bongo at the last possible opportunity. The man refused- until I convinced his young female companion to change his mind.

"Alright, I'll make a deal with you," he said as we drove. "If, by some miracle, we get a bongo this evening, I am going to double the tips I left for everyone."

I mustered a half-hearted smile and shook his hand, telling him we had a deal.

We unenthusiastically dragged our feet to the final salt-lick on the edge of an immense forest. As we neared the high-stand, we could hear splashing down in the mud below us, which gave us a jolt of excitement. Carefully climbing the ladder, we discovered the splashing was coming from a group of Red-River hog. Although the Prince would have gladly taken one of the three beautiful boars in the group- we knew the shot would disturb the forest for dozens of miles around, ruining any chance of a bongo appearing. And so, reluctantly, we let the animals pass, snorting on their way to their secretive night lair deep in the forest.

A troop of baboons appeared next, followed by a rowdy roost of Blue turacos birds. And then, all was silent for the remaining hours of the evening. I went through the usual ranges of emotions in such moments- starting with energetic fantasies of success, the inevitability of success, and finally- hopeless despair. Just as darkness began to engulf the forest, we suddenly heard splashing coming from the muddy salt-lick once again.

It was so dark, when I first pulled up my binoculars, I could not see anything. But the splashing was loud and from a very specific wallow in the center of the salt-lick, I knew it had to be something special. Finally, I made out a body with immense bulk, and on its flanks, those gorgeous white stripes.

"Bongo!" I hissed.

Fumbling, the hunter reached for the rifle and threw it up over the shooting port on the high stand.

"Listen," I said. "We have all the time in the world to take the shot. The animal is in no hurry to leave. Just take your time, and only when its perfect, squeeze the trigger."

Within seconds of the words leaving my mouth, the impatient hunter touched off with a rushed shot, and the forest reverberated with the booming echo of the blast. So quickly had he shot, that I had no time to cover my ears. The ringing in my ears lasted a long time before finally, and gradually, I began to hear the world around me once again. The first thing I could make out was frantic splashing from the center of the salt-lick. Looking down at the dark spot with my binoculars, I saw the bongo flopping around in the mud.

"Shoot it again!" I instructed the client, fearing he might have only stunned the animal with a glancing shot.

The hunter emptied three more rounds toward the animal, but from the rifle's flat report, it sounded like he had missed the three shots completely. Eventually, the animal stopped flopping, and the forest returned to quiet once again.

Everyone was in frenzied excitement as we approached the animal. The man's female companion was hugging the trackers and I. The trackers in turn were slapping the man on his back and lifting him in the air with shouts of celebration.

As we examined the large bull bongo with our flashlights (because it was dark by now), we initially failed to find any bullet holes on the animal's clean bright skin. The client, embarrassed by the thought of missing all those shots, was even more frantic than I to find an answer to this inexplicable question.

"Here," I said, pointing to a tiny hole at the very top of the animal's spine, near the thin tuft of hair running the length of the back.

The bullet had hit so high up, I was shocked that the animal was actually dead and not just stunned by the blow. Upon carefully dissecting the area, we discovered that the bullet had hit the top "fin" of the creature's vertebrae, somehow severing the main spinal nerve upon expansion. A miraculous result for such a bad shot.

The man was clearly embarrassed by this, so I did my best to be a good guide and shower him with congratulations to distract him.

As we drove to the airport the next morning, having successfully collected his main target animal, the man's mood had taken a drastic turn for the better. He was joking with the trackers, smiling and laughing the entire drive; it was the happiest I had seen him during the entire two-week safari. As we neared the airplane, the man took out his wallet in front of everyone. Slowly, while we all sat watching, he pulled out the contents of his wallet, counting each 100-Euro bill. Just when I expected the man to make good on his promise to double our tips- he sheepishly put the contents back in his pocket without ever looking up again.

As he got on the airplane to leave, the Prince of Disaster shook my hand heartily.

"This has been one of my best safaris yet," he said with a beaming smile.

And then, he got on the airplane and left. As the plane flew away, I realized- the fact that the dreadful safari was now over, was the best tip I could have asked for.

Chapter 13: Careful Where You Step

To many Westerners, its easy to imagine the steamy tropical forests of Central Africa are teaming with slithery snakes. In reality, I saw far less snakes than I expected. It was not uncommon for a client to spend two weeks on safari and still not encounter a snake. However, this is not to say one does not have any snake encounters in the bush, especially after spending over 1200 days in the thick of it, like I did. And given the shear variety of venomous specimens that abound, there's a high likelihood any one of those random snake encounters might be of a spicy variety.

During my first-year apprenticeship, the guides in camp would make superstitious jokes about how each of them were assigned "problem animals" in the bush; specific critters that gave them trouble while on safari. For Anton, it was buffalo. During his first season as a guide, he had to shoot a charging bull at point blank range, which managed to graze his hip with its horn. For Erik, it was leopard. Years before, while working in the north of the country, a leopard had climbed a tree in which he and his French client had built a grass blind around, and nearly jumped on top of them while they sat in it.

It was said that my "problem animals" were snakes- since I seemed to encounter them more often than the others. In reality, I was (and am) fascinated by snakes- and many of my encounters occurred because I always kept my eyes peeled for them. Take, for example, my introduction to one of Africa's most notorious serpents.

I was driving around the bush with a young African companion checking on animal activity on local salt-licks, when I thought I saw a snake slither quickly across the road. I stopped the Land Cruiser and jumped out to inspect where the snake disappeared. I was delighted to see the serpent slithering up a nearby tree. When I got to the base of the tree, I took the briefest of moments to inspect the animal. It was olive colored and had a narrow head- but nothing about it looked menacing. I decided to climb the tree to get a closer look. The African man with me groaned and begged me not to pursue the animal. In the Africans' world- all snakes are bad, since misidentifying one might mean certain death.

The snake slowly continued up the tree, apparently ignoring me. I followed the animal, climbing between the labyrinth of tightly growing branches. About the point in my climb when I was too committed to quickly abort, the snake suddenly turned to face me, flaring its neck aggressively like a cobra, and opening its mouth- *its black mouth*.

The only photos I had ever seen of Black mambas were of the very pose I was looking at- and so, I knew without a doubt the identity of this snake. Without taking my eyes off the creature, I halfway fell, halfway scrambled down the tree- scratching my arms and legs badly from the thorns I had previously avoided on my slow ascent.

I would encounter mambas many more times, and in all but one of these encounters, the snakes acted docilely. But that one bad encounter left me forever scared of the creature.

In retrospect, the animal was probably acting defensively in its own way- but from our perspective - the encounter felt like a full-on attack. As we bumped around unawares, the previously unseen snake that was sunning on the road in front of us suddenly reared up and slithered on top of the truck bonnet, striking wildly at the two men sitting on the hood of the truck. The snake came so fast on the vehicle, by the time the two men on the hood and the three of us in the cab had bailed out- the snake was already nearly in the driver's seat. Lucky for us (and unlucky for the snake), the driver had unintentionally struck the snake with his front tire, which broke the animal's back and slowed its attack. The wounded Black mamba attempted to strike multiple people as they exited the vehicle, but one man quickly grabbed a shovel and put the poor animal out of its misery.

Along the main road to the Mbari forest camp, there was a huge Green mamba residing in a tree stump just off the track. The vibrant colors of this snake's body were among the most luxuriant of any animal I had ever seen. This snake became a well-known resident of the area, and we saw it almost every day for two years whenever we passed the spot.

One other snake that has a bad reputation across Africa- but which I grew fond of- was the Puff adder.

The reason for the snake's reputation is that fact that it accounts for more fatal bites than any other snake on the continent. This is because of its far-ranging distribution and high density. They are often found close to human habitation, and end up on collision courses with humans, whether due to bare feet on dark foot-paths, or an errant hand reaching in a pile of firewood.

The reason I grew fond of this snake, is because on more than one occasion, the unseen serpent would warn me of its presence whenever I got too close. On two distinct incidents, I nearly stepped on a Puff adder- which blends in perfectly with the rust-colored leaves of the savanna woodlands in which I often traveled. Both times, the snakes hissed so loud I nearly jumped out of my skin; only to find my foot inches from their mouths. Had they wanted to strike me, they could have done so quite easily. Due to this reason, I made a superstitious truce with the snake; as long as a Puff adder did not strike me, I would never kill one. And it is a truce I have since kept on all my travels in Africa.

Inevitably, if you spend enough time in the bush, you will have unexpected encounters that neither you nor the snake has time to prepare for.

I was on a long, multi-day backpacking trek deep in the forest to investigate a series of salt-licks, when we decided to stop and make camp along a small stream for the night. I was exhausted from the march, and carelessly threw my pack down and dropped on my butt. In a flash, Gambou- my closest African companion- rushed toward me with his machete raised over his head and eyes wild. Instinctively, I threw my arms up to guard my head, momentarily confused and alarmed by his behavior. With a thump, Gambou's machete landed in the mud next to my hip. Between the blade slithered two severed halves of a snake. The creature's skin looked almost ethereal, glowing with vibrant hues of greens and blues; it was a green night adder- a mildly venomous pitless viper with a dangerous bite that would have been catastrophic that far in the bush.

"You have to be careful and keep your eyes open out here!" Gambou chastised me. It was a lesson I wouldn't soon forget.

Another time, while walking in a shin-high forest creek surrounded by thick foliage on either side, I noticed a beautiful Banded water cobra swimming towards me. The lane of travel was small, and the snake stayed its course, despite my splashing steps. Panicking, I tried to backstep and retreat, but the foliage was so thick, I had no clear footing. To my horror, the frightened snake suddenly disappeared in the water, still facing me. I had no idea if it was still under me, had turned right or left, or had retreated the opposite way. Not knowing what to do, I took the only reasonable course of action: I ran out of the water through the leaves on my side, splashing like an elephant in my retreat.

Still another time, I was sitting in a high-stand one evening deep in the forest while on a bongo hunt with an American client. We were only a couple hours into a full-night's stay when I happened to look up in the branches above me and saw a rusty-colored boomslang resting on some delicate branches. My client was especially scared of snakes, and so I did my best not to draw attention to the deadly animal. As the night came on, I found myself obsessively glancing up at the snake, trying to keep tabs on its location. Soon, the whole forest was bathed in darkness, and I spent the entire night obsessing over the whereabouts of the snake. Luckily, it did not pay us a visit in the darkness, and I never saw it again.

I was always delighted to stumble upon African Rock pythons during my adventures in the bush. These animals are non-venomous of course, but their size and coloration make them formidable-looking creatures. During my first road-cutting expedition in the bush, I found a small python resting on some branches above a clear pool of water in which a group of my men were- in that very moment- bathing in. When I reached out and grabbed its tail, the snake suddenly sprang forward and disappeared in the water, sending the group of naked men running in retreat.

Another time, I was having lunch in a small forest during the midday heat, when my companion, Gambou let out a shout. Coming to his aid, I found him frantically pointing up into a tangle of tree vines above us. There, dangling down like a movie-prop, was a medium-sized python, perhaps ten feet in length. Aiming to redeem myself from my last failed attempt to catch a python, I shimmied up the vines like Tarzan, at which point the snake turned and slithered higher into the trees to escape me. I grabbed its tail and pulled hard, sliding my hands farther up its body. When I got control of the animal, it turned its head to face me and let out the most god-awful hiss that only a dragon could have mimicked. This was enough to motivate me to retire from my short python-wrangling career.

While on a foot expedition in the forest, I was accompanied by Gambou and a few other local men, when we emerged onto a salt-lick clearing in the rainforest with a stream of water flowing through the middle. A bushbuck female and its young were sipping water from the stream, when something laying down in front of them caught my attention. It was a large Rock python stalking the young animal, only moments away from striking it! Before I could stop the men, they were hacking the snake into pieces with their machetes, which was a regretful shame. Alas, we ate python meat for dinner that night- a meal that was not unlike fish, but a little less appealing, since the Africans opted to cook it by boiling method, with the scaly skin still attached.

A few days later, on that same expedition, we came upon the rutted tracks in a muddy forest stream that had been made by a monstrous python. If the tracks offered any indication of the snake's size, the creature was a titanic specimen the likes of which might have never been recorded before.

The likelihood of encountering a dangerous snake in the African bush are far lower than most Westerners would probably believe, but this is not to say such encounters won't ever happen. It's important to remain vigilant and keep an eye on where you walk, and be careful what you grab with your hands. That said, if possible, try to make a magical truce with these reptilian neighbors- that way, in the event that you do carelessly blunder into one, they might give you a courtesy warning, like they have me. As for how you might accomplish this truce, that's up to you to figure out.

Chapter 14: *Bongo*, Lord of the Lowland Forest

When I was 10-years-old, my parents took me to the city zoo near my home in Kansas, and this is where I first laid eyes on the mysterious creature that would eventually draw me to Africa: the bongo antelope. To me, it resembled an elk-like animal with black spiral horns and red fur. But the most unbelievable feature was the white stripes running down its flank, like tiger stripes. The rest of my family examined the strange animal for the briefest of moments before moving on to other exhibits; but I remained frozen.

That such a creature could exist in the world was utterly fantastical. It looked like it had just jumped out of a fairytale- completely alien on the Midwestern American soil. I was mystified by the encounter, and it took every effort for my family to remove me from the exhibit.

The impression that sad, imprisoned animal left on me was permanent. For the remainder of my childhood and into my teens, I was obsessed with learning as much as I could about the bongo antelope. I had notebooks full of stories from explorers and hunters alike, and I began to fill up files of bongo pictures from the internet- with one in particular of a running animal taken from National Geographic's Nick Nicholson on a remote salt-lick in the Republic of Congo in 2000.

Fate would lead me to working in the heart of Africa less than a decade later, in a region where the elusive bongo antelope was prevalent.

During my two-year apprenticeship as a Professional Hunter, one of my main tasks was to organize and develop the bongo hunting methods within our company. And so, my road to becoming a Professional Hunter went hand-in-hand with my education on the bongo antelope.

The first time I found a bongo track in sandy gravel bed of a remote forest salt-lick, my heart skipped a beat. I knew immediately the identity of the track the first time I saw it. I bent down and pressed my hand into the impression in a form of reverence for the creature that had inspired so much of my life's dreams. Everywhere I went, cutting new roads and setting up fly-camps, I recorded the bongo activity, and took notes for future reference. Seeing my eager desire to participate in the bongo hunts, Erik gave me the task of scouting out bongo areas and setting up high-stands over forest salt-licks where bongo frequently visited. The fly- camps I set up were incidentally found within the bongo hunting regions of the company's hunting concessions (as opposed to the more common Lord Derby's eland environment of the Sudan-Guinean savanna).

In our hunting area in the eastern Central African Republic, we found through trial and error that hunting with dogs- as is usually common in other places in Africa- was nearly impossible in the dry season when we most often hunted. The ground was not ideal for reliably finding fresh tracks to follow in the mornings, since it hardly ever rained. And the environment itself didn't make hunting with dogs an efficient task, as the bongo habitat here was thick, impenetrable lowland riverine forest. We also wanted to utilize the time we hunted eland to coincide with our ability to hunt bongo. Thus, we found hunting over salt-licks was an ideal method.

Our first real effort at bongo hunting came after one of our trackers- a prolific ex-poacher himself- described to us a very active bongo salt-lick not far from the Mbari river. Erik wasted no time in sending me there to investigate.

Guided by two local hunters, I spent almost a week exploring the bongo forests of the region, including the mythical salt-lick- called Kangaranga- which I was able to confirm, indeed did hold a lot of bongo activity. In fact, the salt-lick had enough activity to prompt Erik into allowing me to organize a bongo hunt there. Returning to the area after my exploratory trip, I brought a convoy of workers and supplies, and we set about preparing our first "bongo camp" along the Mbari river, complimented by a foot path to the salt-lick close by.

The bongo forests in south-eastern CAR look like the kinds of environments one would expect to encounter dinosaurs in. There are many patches of dense shrubs, low-level trees and palms, but occasionally, these areas are broken up by titanic, primary rainforest trees the width of houses and as tall as giant buildings. The forests are scattered like islands held together by spring-fed streams. Many of these streams are crystal clear and can be drank straight from the source. The canopy is occupied by an assortment of aerial wonders, like colorful sun birds, reptile-like Turaco birds, owls and other birds of prey, bats and flying foxes, and hundreds of other brilliantly plumed species. Within the trees live a dozen species of monkey, including the strange Putty-nosed monkey, the Red Colobus, the rare Crowned monkey, and more. On the ground prowl African Golden cats, leopard, giant Rock python, and the more elusive- Gaboon vipers. And the area also includes more iconic species like the Yellow-backed duiker, Giant Forest hog, buffalo, and numerous species of forest duiker.

As I began to explore new salt-licks that Erik had spotted during exploratory fly-overs, I began to learn more about the bongo from "on-the-ground" experience. Some salt-licks had lots of bongo activity, whereas others- no matter how similar in appearance- never had any bongo. Around the salt-licks, on densely forested hillsides, I found bongo tracks and droppings alongside broken and chewed bushes of the slender-leaved Rinorea herbs- indicating a common food source. Around favored bongo entrances on salt-licks, I found what looked like "staging areas," where the animals would remain unseen for a long time, before, presumably, deciding the area was safe before moving into. Learning the shy behavior of the animal and how to hunt them, reminded me of hunting Whitetail deer on crowded public land at home.

Surprisingly, even after spending months in prime bongo habitat, a very long time passed before I actually saw the creatures in the flesh. Whenever Erik had assigned me the work of building fly camps in the bongo areas, I would take advantage of my time there and spend nights alone in the high-stands overlooking the salt-licks, hoping to see the shy antelope. I always carried out these nightly vigils alone.

The time spent in solitude over these salt-licks deep in the rainforest was special. Flocks of exotic Green pigeons and Blue turaco birds fluttered around my head all evening, filling the sky with the most perplexing sounds. As darkness approached, bats would take the place of the birds, fluttering around erratically hunting insects. Monkeys, baboons, bushbuck and even buffalo silently made their appearance on the salt-licks. It was like a lost world in that oasis of open ground, surrounded by dense, primordial jungle.

I spent dozens of nights in these high stands before I ever laid eyes on a bongo in the flesh. Finally, one evening before dark, I watched a fat bongo bull materialize from a thicket on the side of the salt-lick. He looked like a statue, unmoving and weary of the open space- staring out from the edge. When I shifted my gaze for just a moment, the creature was difficult to relocate again- as its striped fur camouflaged it among the rainforest foliage in the approaching darkness. Slowly, methodically, the animal finally moved forward, and I had mere minutes to observe him before darkness completely overtook the place. The image of those twitching ears and tail danced across my dreams that night. The sighting left me on a high for days.

In the years to follow, after finishing my apprenticeship and becoming a licensed PH, I began guiding bongo hunts myself. I found- contrary to popular opinion- sitting over a salt-lick in wait for bongo was never an easy task. Hardly ever were the bongo taken the first night, and on average, a week or more of sitting was required to be successful.

By pure coincidence, one day my entire perception of the bongo as a super-skittish creature almost changed when we bumped into a herd of the animals in the tall grass of the savanna. We watched from a small rise as the animals moved single-file toward a forested area close by- at a distance of no more than 40 yards. It was apparent, out of their dark forest homes where their eyes and ears were adjusted to, they were like fish out of water in the grassland. Interestingly enough, a few ox-pecker birds found the herd in the grass and followed them on their backs like they would buffalo or eland.

As my experience in the region grew, it also became apparent that the bongo in the area had a walking circuit that might encompass a number of salt-licks they visited within a month. Though we knew this was a habit of the animals, predicting when and where they might show up next was almost pure speculation. And not every salt-lick would be visited by bongo on any given night. Some nights the bongo would only visit one salt-lick out of five in the area.

More recently, a large-scale camera trap survey of the area's salt-licks, organized by the manager of the hunting company, David Simpson, confirmed what we had expected about the "bongo walking circuit." But this knowledge didn't make the hunting any easier. Where a bongo might show up on a salt-lick two nights in a row, the same bongo might begin its circuit and visit three other salt-licks in as many nights. It was always a guessing game, with some hunting groups "guessing a bit better." And there were other exceptions.

During my first bongo hunt, I watched as my cheerful, optimistic Texan on day one- turn into a brooding, sleep deprived pessimist by day number eight after we had failed to secure an animal.

Then, finally late one morning, in broad daylight, an ancient bongo bull came strutting out across the largest salt-lick in the area, called Ndolo. Unfortunately, being the largest salt-lick in the area, the bongo was also on the farthest side- too far of a shot for my friend to feel comfortable taking. Oddly, from our position the bongo looked as if he might have lost his horns. Before we could even think or act, the animal disappeared.

We stuck it out in the area, and a couple days later, the same bull appeared; this time, right in front of us. My friend made the shot count, and after two weeks of dedicated bongo waiting- he ended up taking the oldest, most magnificent bongo antelope I had ever seen. One of the animal's horns was completely broken at the base, and the other was snapped three-fourths the way up its remaining spiral horn.

With all the years of experience and observations, we still are finding the only definitive fact we can say for certain of the bongo, is that they are unpredictable. Perhaps no better example of this can be seen than on my very last bongo safari in early 2014.

My client and friend, Ernie, had taken a magnificent Lord Derby's eland on his first day of hunting, and a couple days later, a nice buffalo bull. I wanted to keep the momentum of good luck by enticing him to try for bongo; but at first, Ernie declined. Having accomplished more than what he had come for, he was now content just to sit back and enjoy the rest of the trip. Finally allowing the carefree mindset to replace any stress I might have carried to produce results, I too enjoyed the leisurely time.

One of the last days of the safari, we were driving around in the bush with no set schedule, no set destination, and above all- no set plan. We had brought a lunch kit with us in case we found a nice spot to park our Land Cruiser for a tropical siesta. At some point during the drive, we arrived next to one of the thick forest areas in the concession. Inside was a high-stand above a salt-lick that many species of animal would visit during the day. Most of these furry residents were of the pig variety- like Red River hogs or Giant Forest hog, and occasional buffalo; only on the rarest of occasions did bongo visit that salt-lick. This particular one was muddy, small, and in close proximity to a savanna plateau; It just didn't seem like the kind of salt-lick bongo generally preferred. Arriving to the spot, I offered to have our picnic inside the carefully built tree-stand, and Ernie readily agreed.

The forest was much cooler than the outside savanna. After a quiet meal and a session of bird-watching, the bubbling spring creek below us began to lull us to sleep. With birdsong all around and rays of sunlight shimmering through the leaves, I was about to enter dream land, when suddenly- my ears began to pick up on something. It was a faint sound that wasn't there before; something moving slowly through the forest. Ernie and I both sat up, listening.

A stand of gargantuan forest leaves began to shake just on the edge of the mineral lick. Suddenly, a large blazing red creature appeared; its thick horns curved toward the sky and white stripes cut down its flanks- Bongo! For the first time in the five years I had hunted in Central Africa, I was watching a bongo bull moving at 2pm in the middle of the day. It was absurd- simply maddening. The high-stand was suddenly charged with electric energy.

Wide-eyed, I handed the .375 H&H to Ernie, who- equally wide eyed- grabbed the rifle without hesitation. He positioned the firearm as slow as he could before readying his aim. There was a moment of silence, as we took in the special encounter and watched the bongo bull feed. Sweat dripped from Ernie's face, and his muscles eased as he pulled the trigger. The peaceful calm of the forest was suddenly jarred by the shot.

The trackers came hurrying down to the salt-lick after hearing the shot. At the sight of the animal, they shouted with joy; none of us had expected to see this precious creature here, in the middle of the day. I too was caught up in the emotional celebration, and we all sang and admired the bull loudly. My legs quivered, and adrenaline pulsed through my body as I knelt down and examined the impressive creature. All the emotions I had first experienced when I came to Central Africa in search of the mythic creature suddenly came rushing back.

This was the reason I had come to Africa.

Chapter 15: The Three Not-so-little Pigs

Three different wild pig species can be found in Sub-Sahara Africa: the famous Warthog, which needs no introduction. The Red River hog of central and south-east Africa, and the Giant Forest hog of Central Africa. Each of these species have distinctly unique physical features and occupy their own niche habitats.

The Warthog has gray, leathery skin with a scattering of a few coarse hairs and a horse-like mane. Grotesque nodules shoot off the creature's face, and the mature males sport large, curving white ivory teeth that typically grow like a steering-wheel on the front of their faces. These animals occupy more of the dry savanna and woodland habitats, although they can be found in almost any landscape south of the Sahara.

The Red River hog sports brilliant red fur with a contrasting white stripe down its back. Its elf-like ears dangle from the side of its head, giving it a novel, almost fairy-tale appearance. Unlike most pig species, the Red River hogs have an almost sweet-smelling musk. They occupy tropical wetlands where thick cover is available.

Giant Forest hog are- as their name suggests- a giant of a pig species. They are hulking jet-black creatures that can grow x4 times as large as their two African cousins, up to 600lbs. Large disk-like glands sprout from their chubby faces, and only the largest males and females have ivory nubs that pop out the sides of their mouths. They occupy the densest forests in Central Africa, but can on occasion venture out into the transitional habitats on the forest-edge.

Although there are a few places in Africa where the three species can be found living alongside one another, the Chinko basin is- as far as I am concerned- one of the only places where one can consistently expect to see them; sometimes in the same day. On more than one occasion my hunting clients were able to harvest all three species in one week's time. One of these hunts stands out to me because of how incredible each of the encounters were.

The client was a young man from southern Asia in his late 20s, and it was an unusual and pleasant experience to hunt with a client so close to my own age. Owing to his youthful vigor and stamina, we were able to hunt harder than would typically allow with older clients. This made for an enjoyable experience for everyone.

When hunting out of our main camp along the Kocho river in the savanna woodlands, it was common for us to check a nearby salt-lick we called *Kava*, due to the stand of massive, white-barked trees that grew there- known locally as Kava trees. After having spent my two-year apprenticeship irresponsibly shooting every warthog I saw around camp (either for purposes of acquiring leopard bait or pre-season meat for the workers), I grew to appreciate how rare and elusive a big, mature warthog was. Their tusks, like elephants, take many years to grow; so a warthog with big tusks was guaranteed to be ancient. And with so many predators about, growing old as a warthog was no small task.

Imagine my surprise then, when after parking the truck some distance away and slowly approaching the Kava salt-lick on foot, we were shocked to spot a large-tusked Warthog boar with a group of females just off to the side- in a place I had driven by hundreds of times without ever seeing such an animal.

Now I won't exaggerate the efforts normally required to take a Warthog in Africa; as anyone who has ever hunted on the continent knows, they don't take their self-preservation too seriously when standing in front of men with rifles. And although they do run when approached, they often take their time in doing so. However, for better or worse, this particular Warthog was different.

As soon as we noticed the animal, he was on to us and took off into a cluster of shrubs with his tail sticking in the air like an antenna. We scurried around the stand of shrubs hoping to intercept the now unseen animal. But like a magician, when we got there, we found the warthog standing defiantly in front of a stand of low trees, 200-yards distant- much too far for the animal to have traveled so quicky. As we swiveled to take the shot, the animal disappeared into the trees.

We rushed forward once again trying to intercept the animal. A deep ravine stretched below the stand of trees where the boar disappeared, and I feared we would lose it forever; a maddening thought to consider- to be outwitted by a warthog. When we reached the spot where the pig should have been, again, we found emptiness. Only the ravine with an impenetrable thicket stretched in front of us, and I knew we could never follow the pig in there. Sheepishly, I abandoned what I had anticipated would be an easy chase, and we started the long walk back to the truck.

With our heads held low in defeat, we were nearing the truck when I looked up, astonished to see the boar standing next to the vehicle. The shock almost prevented me from moving the shooting sticks into position, and I had barely any time to point out the pig to the client before it was off again. Luckily, the young hunter dropped the warthog with a running shot, securing his first wild pig species of the safari. Had our truck not been parked in the perfect location of the pig's escape, we would have never seen it again.

It was a beautiful boar with tusks wrapped in a perfectly symmetrical circle. In that moment, we were focused on eland, and didn't consider this might be the start of the lucky hunter's "pig slam" (taking all three species in one safari). The hunter was simply happy to secure a good representative of the iconic African animal.

My young hunter had never seen a Red River hog on his previous safaris in Africa, and he had no desire to take one... until he encountered them one evening early in the hunt.

We found the herd of pigs with three big boars crossing a recently burned patch of open ground on their way from one forest to another forest. Because the ground was open and covered in black ash, the animal's red fur contrasted sharply against the dark backdrop, making them look an even brighter red than usual. My client took one look at the magical animals and became completely fixated on them. We took off running across the flat landscape, eager to reach the animals before they disappeared into the forest they were now only a few seconds away from. I threw the shooting sticks up and told the man to shoot, but it was a hopeless endeavor. The poor man's face was purple and he was gasping for air from our unplanned sprint. He tried to steady the rifle on the sticks, but they just danced wildly with each gasping breath. He shot and missed. Then shot again and missed. He kept shooting- through two more re-loads- missing each time. At a certain point, I stepped back and quietly let the poor man take out his frustration with more than a half-a-dozen missed shots.

After the blunder, the man became obsessed with taking the elfin-like Red River hog for the remainder of the safari. But as is usually the case, after over a week of searching, we never found any more.

Our lucky break came when we were least expecting it. After a failed stalk on a herd of buffalo, we decided to sit just inside the shade of a forest to take a break. This particular forest was known to grow wild peppercorn- more flavorful than any I had ever eaten. The men set off to forage for the treats nearby.

Allen, the youngest tracker, suddenly appeared from deeper in the forest a few minutes later and hurried over to me excitedly.

"Red River hog!" he whispered, "Working their way through the stream just below us."

I grabbed the client and we followed Allen hurriedly to where the two other trackers awaited us. Charles, the lead tracker, guided us quietly but quickly through the tangle of forest until we came to a thicket on the edge of a small stream, and it was here we set up our ambush. The clear water suddenly ran muddy, as debris from the pig's disturbance upstream drifted down toward us. Then, came the snorting and splashing of the approaching pigs. We all held our breath in eager anticipation, as red forms began to appear in flashes between the gaps in the lush green foliage. It seemed like the animals would approach to within a few feet of us.

But something happened. The animals, which had been on a course straight toward us, suddenly turned up the creek bank and began foraging on a dry hillside opposite of us, now unseen in the thick forest. No good. We backed out of there and made a quick loop outside of the forest and then back in just ahead, where we hoped to intercept the animals again. Our nerves and adrenaline at the close encounter were at their highest as we set up our second ambush. But again, the pigs turned at the last moment and took a different route. Frustratingly, they were following the same direction of the flowing creek, but the forest was too wide to anticipate exactly where their finicky route would take them.

We exited the forest once again and moved ahead to cut the animals off. This time, I spotted what seemed like a narrower funnel in the riverine forest. I pushed the team forward to the spot. We were now very far from where we had lost the animals, and doubts began to creep up. From our location, the animals might have completely left the forest, and we would never know it.

Suddenly, the dry leaves on the forest floor began to crackle with dozens of shuffling pig steps approaching us. Without any time to move, a line of females and young appeared in front of us. Charles was point-man, I behind him, the client to my right, and the two other trackers behind me. The animals appeared so suddenly and so closely, we could do nothing but freeze. But to my utter relief, the young hunter had his rifle up and aiming in the direction of the animals.

"Wait until I tell you to shoot," I said quietly.

When I say the animals appeared in front of us- I mean, literally in front of us, appearing in the small gap in the thicket that we now sat in. Each animal moved in a single file across from us so close, my hunter could have leaned forward and touched them with the end of his .375 H&H. I had never been so close to Red River hog before.

Finally, a large and gnarled old boar appeared in the line, and when he came in front of the hunter's barrel, I told him, "Shoot!"

Rarely have I seen a sportsman follow an instruction so calmly in such an excitable situation as that. With one shot through the lungs, the animal dropped stone dead. Unfortunately, all of us were bunched close together and had no time to cover our ears for the loud percussion of the shot. Poor Charles' head was inches from the end of the rifle barrel, and the impact on his eardrums was painful enough to send him on the ground in a fetal position moaning in pain.

Normally, hunting wild pigs in Africa offers an unremarkable side quest to the more exciting pursuits of the charismatic larger fauna; but this particular hunt turned out to be one of the most exciting pursuits of any hunt I had experienced among any species.

After taking photos, my men carefully cut and stripped tree-vine ropes and lashed the animal's feet and hand together over a sturdy sapling. Together, we hoisted the animal in the air, and the five of us walked single-file out of the forest together, struggling under an even load through the tangled tree roots and thickets. When we emerged onto the savanna above the forest, we were all covered in sweat and feeling contentedness only truly appreciated through hard work. It would be the largest, most impressive Red River hog any of my hunters would ever take in my career.

Toward the end of the safari, after bagging a big Lord Derby's eland, buffalo, numerous duikers, and a collage of other unique animals found endemic to the area- my hunter was feeling pretty content with himself. Joining us one day was a visiting PH from Zimbabwe, a man named Pete Wood. Pete had just arrived that season to guide safaris in our northern hunting concession, and he wanted to tag along and get acquainted with the Chinko valley.

Pete must have brought some extra good luck that day, because what followed was a Giant Forest hog hunt the likes of which I would never experience again.

We drove toward the southern end of the Chinko river, near the confluence of the Kocho river. We were in no pursuit of a set species, simply enjoying the end of an already successful safari. Along the way, we shot some Crested guinea fowl with my camo painted 12-gauge "leopard" shotgun. This made a delicious meal for us along the Chinko river itself, where we grilled the plucked birds over an open fire, seasoned to perfection by our chef- the young tracker, Allen. Most of the day was uneventful in way of animal sightings, but we were enjoying ourselves none-the-less. Because we weren't actively searching for target species that day, we were enjoying the scenery at a leisurely pace.

I knew of a particularly scenic rocky pinnacle overlooking the Chinko river as it snaked its way toward the hazy horizon. As it was nearing sunset, I decided to take the group here for a sundowner. We left the Land Cruiser a couple hundred yards away and walked up the dry rocky approach to the top of the overlook. As usual, the evening left a beautiful orange glow across the vast expanse stretching toward Chad and Sudan, and we paused to enjoy the moment.

Suddenly, Pete cried out in his deep, excitable Zimbabwean accent, "Giant Forest hog!"

I followed the direction of his pointing finger, and found an unbelievable scene: a group of Giant Forest hog feeding on the lush green shrubs growing along the Chinko river itself. Here, the water flowed crystal clear on bright granite boulders banked on either side by clean white sand. The black fur of the animals stood out even more darkly against the sand, making them appear larger and more impressive than usual.

Not only was this the client's first sighting of the rare and elusive Giant Forest hog, but it was also Pete Wood's first encounter with the animals. Having guided all over Africa, this was Pete's first time hunting Central Africa's endemic wildlife, and he knew just how special this animal was. His excitement was contagious.

"Let's go take that big male!" he said pumping the shoulders of my young client. My hunter paused and was about to respond in protest, but Pete wouldn't take no for an answer.

"You might not ever see this animal again in this setting!" he said to the man, "Now let's go!"

We scrambled down the small peak behind Pete's heals, moving from large granite boulder to the next, stalking the hogs that were feeding unaware on the other side of the river. I stepped back and let the excited Pete take the lead, pushing the hunter forward with my shooting sticks and getting the man in position to shoot.

The shot itself was unremarkable, and the boar dropped stone dead on the banks of the opposite side of the river without any trouble. It was the setting of the hunt that was so special. We had explored the banks of the Chinko for years and had only rarely seen animals-occasionally hippo or waterbuck. The river itself was a highway for the remaining Sudanese Janjaweed ivory poachers, and the animals learned to avoid its banks. This was the only time I have ever seen Giant Forest hog on the river itself.

After taking our boots off and carefully scanning around for crocodiles in the deeper pools, we forded the shallow water single-file. Darkness was quickly approaching, and out of necessity, we hurried the process of taking photos and gutting the pig. By the time we had lashed the large animal on a sapling and struggled back across the river together, it was sufficiently dark enough now that the water was completely black. We knew there were deep pools of water both upstream and downstream of us, and I cringed at the thought of what might be lurking around us now that the water was too dark to see anything.

In my short career as a PH, a handful of my clients were able to secure a "pig slam," taking all three species of wild boars found in

Central Africa. However, no ending to a pig slam would ever compare in adventure to ours that night, when we crossed the Chinko river loaded down by a big Giant Forest hog boar.

Chapter 16: A Safari of my Own

At the closing of my second season as a Professional Hunter, I would undertake an adventure that my younger self would have only believed to be a dream: I would lead my own personal hunting safari deep in the African bush.

As was usually the case when I hunted for myself and not with paying clients, this hunt was conducted in coordination with a road cutting expedition into new territory. Only this time, I would pay for the hunting licenses of larger, more special animals than the standard duiker and baboon that I typically hunted. Namely, I was hoping to collect a buffalo on my own, and- if the stars aligned- a Yellow-backed duiker.

We cut this new road between the Ngoy and Mbari rivers, in an acacia woodland occasionally broken by thin forest galleries. It was a place one could expect to find savanna species like eland, buffalo, and roan; but also, an unexpectedly high density of certain forest species like Giant Forest hog and Yellow-backed duiker. We had to ford a number of rivers on this trip, but these were not like the densely forested rivers found in most places in the hunting block, but were open and characterized by wide sand banks. When following these watercourses, I was blown away by the sheer number of broken clay pottery pieces that made up the gravel beds. How old these artifacts were was anyone's guess; but that they were ancient was clear, considering there was no recorded history- oral or otherwise- of anyone occupying this place.

The expedition took a few long weeks to complete, and incidentally, we encountered various groups of buffalo. Even though I had a license for buffalo, I was still busy managing the road cutting work. And so, every time I left the men to their tasks, my foreman Mattheo and I would set off as a pair to hunt. We would only have a couple of hours of free time available before we had to return to the work. This made it challenging to actually connect with an animal.

It was empowering to be able to track buffalo on my own, without my team of expert trackers by my side. But this also meant I tracked at a much slower pace. Despite the game-rich area, my time for hunting was limited. I did manage to get within shooting distance of a nice herd bull one day after a long tracking job. But as I crawled through dry yellow grass and eased behind a termite mound, readying for the shot- the wind suddenly turned and blew straight at the animals, sending them stampeding away. I was so close to finally shooting a bull, that the sudden failure was a crushing blow, and I became discouraged at the prospect of ever taking a shot.

My luck did eventually come one morning, after a light rain the night before had softened the ground, making it easier to track. As Mattheo and I continued forward scouting the new road ahead, we came to a forest crossing and began pushing through the dense undergrowth, searching for a path to the other side. Just then, the wall of greenery right below us exploded with retreating animals. We waited for the commotion to subside, and then watched as a small herd of buffalo came pouring out of the forest opposite of us. This was my chance.

We gave the animals time to calm down, and then crossed the forest as quietly as possible, and began to track the herd where they had exited on the other side. As luck would have it, the animals were not too spooked, and they began to feed almost immediately after they had exited. As I stalked closer to the animals, I noted a large bull feeding close to us, at less than 100 yards. Realizing my shot opportunity was about to finally happen, my heart started beating uncontrollably and I struggled to breathe.

Up to this point, I had guided many buffalo hunts, but I was always the backup shooter for my client in those situations, and never the one to take the first shot myself. Now, with the rifle in my hands, I felt humbled by the shear intimidation I felt- and I vowed to never judge a nervous client too harshly ever again in such a situation.

The bull began feeding toward me and then turned broadside at 80 yards. Resting the rifle in the crook of a tree, I aimed the iron sights of the .458 Lott right at the shoulders, took a deep breath, then pulled the trigger. At the shot, the bull hunched over in pain, but then regained its strength enough to take off in a sprint. Seeing that the animal was running toward the dense cover of the forest, I quickly sent three more bullets into it, tipping it over with the last shot. When I approached the fallen beast after giving it a long time to expire, I found two of those follow-up shots had hit the animal in the heart, less than an inch away from each other.

After gutting and quartering the bull with Mattheo- a daunting task for only the two of us- we set off to fetch the rest of the road cutting crew. On the way back, we accidentally stumbled on a magnificent salt-lick flanked by a thin circle of forest. I marked the spot on my GPS and vowed to return there as soon as possible. It would take all of us in the road cutting crew, each carrying our own heavy load of meat over a mile in a cold thunderstorm, before we could finally make it back to our camp late at night. We smoked the meat over the course of two days while the road work continued.

Nearly a week went by since I had shot the buffalo, and no free time had permitted me to return to the salt-lick that now taunted my imagination. Our new hunting road stretched far, and we finally came to our fourth creek crossing. Our work slowed from there, and since I had sent back much of the buffalo meat to main camp, we were now running low for our own protein supply. Seizing the opportunity to hunt one morning, I left the others to work on the crossing, and set off towards the salt-lick with one of my trackers, Charles.

No sooner had we crested a small hill above the salt-lick, when we caught sight of our destination, and multiple animals moving around it. My heart leaped. My suspicions had proved true. We quickly checked the wind, and adjusted our route of direction. We carefully worked our way down into a patch of trees and were soon at the edge of the salt-lick opening, where we were finally able to make out the animals. It was a herd of seven Giant Forest hogs, and there was a big, ancient male in the middle.

The Giant Forest hog is an elusive forest species. It is its secrecy that makes it little known to the outside world. Everyone knows mister Warthog, but for whatever reason, the Forest hog has not quite become as famous as his piggy cousin. They are by far the biggest swine species in Africa, and perhaps the most difficult for hunters to target specifically; but here, in the forest galleries of the Central African Republic, the animals thrive.

At a distance of about 150 yards from the animals, I instructed Charles to stay down, as I advanced alone, moving painstakingly slowly. The salt-lick was like a massive bowl of mucky pudding, and after closing the distance a further 50 yards, I had efficiently muddied my entire legs and arms. The pigs were now moving around nervously, and the wind was starting to waver.

Giant Forest hogs are famous for their poor eyesight and hearing, but with their moose sized noses, whatever other senses they may lack, their sense of smell makes up for it. I could tell I had only a moment to take a shot at the old boar before they would all disappear. There were no trees around to take a steady shot, so I quickly rose to a squatting prone position. With my arms solid against my knees, I took aim with the open-sighted .458 Lott and squeezed the trigger. The shot, although somewhat risky, worked far better than I could have imagined. The boar dropped dead in his tracks and needed no second shot.

To my surprise, immediately after the boar dropped, an old she-devil pig standing behind the male let out a furious squeal before rushing upon her fallen mate. In a split second she was on top of his limp body, thrashing about his stomach with her sharp tusks, and letting out her revenge for whatever abuse she had received from the old boy during their courtship. Even while the five other pigs were long gone, she continued to batter the old boar. It was only when Charles and I walked within 20 yards of her did she hightail it out of there.

Attracted by the sound of the shot, the entire camp turned up on the salt-lick within a matter of minutes. We all took our time admiring the old beast. One tusk was completely broken off right under the top lip, and the other tusk was mostly worn down to a point. Large, splayed scars ran a fair length down its rump; a lion's failed attempt to secure a fat meal I assumed. The boar was much older and grander than I had previously judged, and it was clear, in such harsh environments he would not have lasted many more seasons.

That evening, we spent a lazy time in camp, mostly smoking large portions of the meat over open fires. For dinner, we had a delicious meal of deep-fried pork cuts, complimented with rice and tomato sauce. The meal was a greasy, delicious one, and a welcome change to the stale, dry buffalo meat we had been eating the last couple of weeks. After dinner, we all sat by campfires, sipping on delicious homemade honey wine that had been fermenting for the last couple of days.

Up to that point, I felt very content with the previous week's hunting opportunities. As our work environment changed from thick forest areas to open savannahs and rolling hills, my hopes for taking a Yellow-backed duiker were now gone. Still, every day Mattheo would assure me that before our road work ended, I would have my chance at the rare animal. Although a very positive prophecy, with only a few days of work left, I highly doubted his prediction would come true. And in any case, I had just taken my first Central African savanna buffalo on my own, and a magnificent old Giant Forest hog boar; for even a seasoned hunter, I couldn't ask for more.

On a crystal clear morning, I set off to mark up the last eight miles of road I was assigned to finish. The job would be complete in no more than three days. It was my very last task of the season. After that, I would head back to main camp for a couple of days, then back to Bangui before flying home to Kansas City. I casually walked on, already back home mentally. Seven months of work in the bush was now leaving me with little motivation to continue on with the last couple of days of road cutting. I was staring at the ground for a long time, when I caught movement to my left in a small patch of trees about 50 yards away.

I looked up slowly and simultaneously pulled up the .223 rifle I was carrying. Some medium sized animal took off at a fast trot, angling away and to my right. There were too many bushes in the way to identify it. Whatever it was, it looked dark, almost black. My heart began to race, but I didn't want to give my hopes up quite yet. I hurriedly ran parallel to the animal, desperately trying to see what it was.

And then it stopped. In a small clearing, illuminated by a ray of morning sunlight, stood a large Yellow-backed duiker; and far from any large forest! My insides exploded with anxiety. And it took all my discipline to control my shaking arms long enough to pull up the rifle and make the shot. I coached myself mentally: *Aim. Squeeze the trigger…*

And so I did. The animal dropped at the shot.

I felt a mixture of elation and sorrow as I walked up to the magnificent animal. I touched the short, stubbly fur on its neck, and ran my hand down the long, course yellow fur on its back. The culmination of a full season's work, and three years of searching in vain, and now a fine Yellow-backed duiker lay at my feet. The rainy season had recently started, and fresh new grass made the backdrop to my most prized hunting photo. It was a fitful ending to a long and memorable adventure.

I stayed awake all night preparing the duiker skin, with the dedicated help of two of my workers. It was late by the time we had completely skinned and fleshed out the hide. Sometime, shortly after we had completed our task, a hyena let out a cry under the moonlight. It sounded very close to our camp. One of the Africans awoke and yelled to me to keep an eye on the skin, lest the scavenger should take it.

But he didn't even have to tell me. I was already on guard, leaning against a tree with flashlight and rifle in hand. I would stay up all night if I had to. I had cut over 50 miles of road, slept on the ground for three weeks, and endured plenty of other hardships - nothing, not even a mischievous hyena could take away my prize from me now.

Chapter 17: The Hunters

I have known a lot of lands intimately, from the Midwest Whitetail woodlots of my youth, to the Rocky Mountains out West; from the old-world forests of eastern Europe, to the distant Arctic Circle in Alaska. Out of all of these places, Africa feels different- and I'm not talking about the obvious physical differences. One can sense, almost intuitively, that Africa is older than other places.

Africa's oldness is ineffable and omnipresent. It is felt everywhere across the continent- in its dark forests, its barren deserts, and its violent grasslands; in its lazy reptilian rivers, and its sun scorched woodlands. When traveling on foot in the African bush- one always carries a sense of expectancy; an inevitable encounter yet to manifest itself. *What is that over there, shaking behind those bushes?*

In the eastern Central African Republic, on the frontier to one of the largest wildernesses left in Sub-Saharan Africa, stretching for hundreds of miles into South Sudan- small settlements of people exist. These people are made up of a collage of scattered lineage: Banda, Nzakara, Baya, Nzande, and even Fulani Arabs. These people straddle two worlds: one in which modern comforts of cell phones and internet service are easily obtainable, and the other in which a subsistence existence is necessary. These people are as old as the lands they occupy.

The hunter class of people that live among these outposts of civilization are as quiet and unassuming as the ancient lands in which they live. Their women harvest crops in their semi-feral "bush" gardens, while the men set off in the wilderness with their homemade shotguns in search of game. Most often they will go on day trips, hunting duiker and birds or checking snares. Other times, well planned *grande chasse* hunting expeditions are conducted, in which a handful of the best hunters of a community will set off in a convoy with supplies for a week or more, checking game trails and salt-licks their fathers and grandfathers had hunted before them deep in the bush. If successful, they will return home after many days and nights afield, loaded with hundreds of pounds of smoked meat. Game collected can come in the form of buffalo, Giant Forest hog, bongo antelope, Yellow-backed duiker- or any other animal that might come in their way.

When the rare elephant wanders near a community, the local hunters will drop what they are doing and set off in pursuit. Often, they might only be wearing flipflops and carry a machete, an old colonial rifle, matches, a little food, and the meagerest of supplies- with no way of knowing when or if they might catch up to the large quarry.

When foreign sport hunters come to Africa, their safaris usually rank high on their list of many adventurous accomplishments. The well-organized and fairly comfortable experiences are memorialized in the trophies they bring home and hang on their walls, the awards they earn from exclusive hunting clubs, and through documentary photography. These hunters are often quite vocal about their excursions, promoting their prowess as venerate sportsman far and wide to whomever might listen to them.

Meanwhile, the lowly African trackers working in the shadows of these safaris speak little about their own hunting experiences in the bush; experiences that would make the foreign hunters' safaris look like a walk in the zoo in comparison. In the eastern Central African Republic, the local hunters often carried out epic feats of valor that would be celebrated in contemporary art and film had their stories been told in another era. And yet, due to the circumstances of their obscurity, these adventures pass with unremarkable consistency.

Profiles of Legendary Trackers

Any story I share about legendary African trackers wouldn't be complete without the names of Bienvenue and Mongolor. Though they were childhood mates from the same town of Fode and would grow up hunting elephants deep in the African bush together, the two men couldn't be any different in nature. Mongolor was fiery and intense, while Bienvenu was calm and friendly.

Mongolor was a wiry and intense man; his pupils were the color of Tiger's-eye gem, and they flashed the only two extremes of his emotion: intensely happy, or intensely angry. When considering sheer skill level alone, he was the best tracker CAWA safaris had. The only problem was, he was a hothead who could not be managed successfully by anyone- save for Erik.

Upon first meeting Mongolor, one immediately notices the ghastly scar running diagonally across his face- between eyeballs, down the bridge of nose, and ending straight across the cheek. This, he received from a wounded leopard he decided to pursue in the thick forests of the Mbari, after a young member of his hunting party had shot and lost it. He hadn't made it very far into the thicket before the cat pounced and had its hook-shaped claws latched onto his scalp while its hind legs worked furiously to disembowel him. Somehow, he managed to get his knees to his chest and push the cat outwards with his feet while touching off with a snapshot from his shotgun. This successfully broke the engagement with the leopard; unfortunately, the wrestling match with the cat had resulted in Mongolor's scalp being torn loose and flung over his face, temporarily blinding him.

Had this story not made him famous in the region due to the noticeable scar it left across his face, his other run-ins with dangerous animals would have brought equal attention. Like the time he got knocked unconscious by a charging buffalo, which managed to smash his skull with the hard boss of its own skull. Or the other time, when a wounded bongo antelope charged him and sent a horn into his leg. On another hunting expedition, an elephant had sent a tusk through the guts of a man in the party, and it was Mongolor who used a fishing line to sew the man's stomach shut after having to push the intestines back in place (this story was corroborated by numerous men I met).

Bienvenu, Mongolor's childhood friend, also wears a permanent souvenir from his hunting adventures.

Upon meeting the open, round-faced man, one immediately notices his shriveled and crooked right arm. During a *grande chasse* deep in the Mbari-Bonga forests, Bienvenue and his fellow hunters tracked a herd of elephant into a forested rocky outcrop and began to lay waste to the animals with their rifles- a combination of ancient .375 Holland and Hollands and AK-47s. A cornered cow elephant guarding its calf charged the line of men, singling out Bienvenue. As it bore down on him, he fell, and the enraged cow began to trample him, pushing down on his chest with its trunk and head, trying to mash him into the ground. In the process, one of the cow's foot stomped his arm, crushing the bone into splinters. The wounded cow was eventually killed, and the gravely wounded man was carried back to the village.

Ironically, the most harrowing part of the ordeal- according to Bienvenu- was the months of recovery following the attack. A witch doctor did his best to put the exposed splintered bones back in place through a massive gash that had opened on his forearm. Then, a collection of medicinal plants were shoved into the cavity and sinched shut. For weeks the man writhed in feverish pain in his grass roofed hut, until slowly he began to recover.

Bienvenu would take me to those hollowed grounds where the attack took place, many, many years after the event. I stood on the rocky outcrops within the shady shelter of the dry forest as a light wind blew the tall trees rhythmically, trying to imagine the violence and chaos of that day. In that moment, I was struck with the sheer silence of it all: not just the forest, but the life of the whole region. Poaching had ravaged the elephant population there, and the memory of their presence lingered only within the stories of people like Bienvenue and the scar he wore on his arm.

In a twist of fate, Bienvenue would go on to become one of the most distinguished wildlife rangers of the newly established Chinko Preserve- going on to protect the remnant elephant population he once hunted, now helping them regain a footing in the region.

My First Mentor

George was my first real mentor in the hunting business, and a perfect example of one who straddles the two worlds of the modern and ancient. He grew up in northern CAR and hunted for bush meat in a bygone era when the area still held Black rhinoceros, giraffe, cheetah and more. Later, he became a tracker for a number of hunting outfits, before doing a stent as an anti-poaching ranger against the notoriously violent ivory poachers from Sudan. When I met him, he was one of very few licensed Professional Hunters of Central African nationality.

George was a small, old man when I met him, no more than 5'3" and probably 130lbs. On his chest, just below his solar plexus, he carried a ghastly scarred indention the size of a baseball. This crude souvenir was given to him by a wounded buffalo. One of the most remarkable aspects of George as a hunting mentor, was the fact that when I met him, he had not killed any living creature in decades- and refused to shoot even a bird for supper. His years as an anti-poaching ranger had weighed heavy on him; he had killed numerous men in the bush, and the killings took their toll on his psyche. When he retired from the gruesome work, he vowed never to kill another creature knowingly.

Even though George was a licensed guide, he did not know English, which made it difficult for him to interact with many of our Western clients. It was Erik's idea then to have George act as a lead tracker and guide during my first safaris, in order to better help me learn the entire process. In this way, I could learn how to "guide" hunts, while having George as a mentor in the background.

Most of my mentorship with George took place under unremarkable circumstances. I would watch him carefully as he followed the obscure tracks left by a herd of eland or buffalo we were following. He didn't even need to lower his head when he tracked; he simply held a small stick out in front of him with his head held straight, and bounced the stick up and down in the air, in quiet acknowledgment of each footprint his eyes followed. While we pursued the animals, he would silently point out obscure sign, or make a quiet comment about the animals' behavior. Little by little, I absorbed this information.

One memory stands out to me the most from my time with George, and it was during one of my first buffalo hunts, when I had very little experience with both my .458 Lott rifle and using it against dangerous game. While stalking a herd one day, we were walking over a small rise when the wind changed directions and turned straight into the mass of animals, sending them thundering away in retreat. We all let our guard down in that moment, thinking the animals had completely disappeared. Suddenly, a protective she-buffalo came boiling out of the brush in front of us. I looked on in horror as the furious animal emerged a couple yards from George- who calmly and casually knelt down and then curled up in a ball behind a basketball-sized termite mound. Meanwhile, my European client and the other two trackers turned to run.

The sight was absurd: the 130lb George was curled up in a ball on the ground with only a quarter of his body mass hidden behind a lump of dirt, while a 2,000lb buffalo was snorting angrily and stomping a dust cloud in the air in semi-circles around him.

By now, my rifle was trained on her, and I could just make out George's face peeking out at me from his fetal position. My heart was in my throat, and I thought I was going to have to shoot the animal –

which would have no doubt fell on top of George. The buffalo, confused by the human ball in front of her and the chaos of the retreating hunting party behind me- stammered for a moment before turning away indignantly, nose in the air.

When she left, I lowered my shaky arms and nearly collapsed from the weight of the adrenaline dump. George simply stood up, shook the dust off his pants, and let out a carefree chuckle.

"Merci beaucoup," he said, walking up to me with a big smile before patting me on the shoulder, acknowledging my ready rifle. Apparently, he had more confidence in my ability to protect him than I did in myself.

George had a tough life even beyond his years as an aggressive anti-poaching ranger. His wife bore him four children- and the last I heard from him, only two survived into adulthood. George would be kidnapped by the infamous LRA rebels during the later years of our safari outfit in Chinko, and would endure weeks of brutal conditions and beatings before he would escape, half-starved and covered in wounds. When the civil war broke out in 2013, fighting in the north of the country where he lived was especially intense. I do not know if George survived the civil war in the Central African Republic, but I always think about the man and what he taught me.

My African Brotherhood

The name that most often appears in my stories is that of Gambou. Although he was my same age and acted only as my second tracker during hunting safaris, no other person in Africa made a more formidable impression on me than he. We became more than working colleagues- we became close friends. He was not the best hunter or tracker that I would meet, but he was the best teacher- patiently explaining everything he did while on the hunt or practicing bushcraft. Through careful assimilation of his instructions, I would grow to move about the bush with ease. I could pull hundreds of stories about Gambou from the wellspring of memory, but for the sake of time, I'll share only one.

During my first year as an apprentice, Gambou and I were tasked with cutting a long network of foot paths through a dense forest close to the main camp. The trail would act as a location to take clients on foot hunts for forest species without having to venture far into the bush. As it turned out, the unassuming location would hold much adventure for us in the years to come.

We spent three days cutting the trail. As usual, Gambou and I set off ahead marking the path while a handful of workers came behind us, clearing it properly with axes and machetes. It didn't take long for the two of us to leave the men behind and penetrate deep in the forest, where the sound of the working men soon ceased.

It took time to carefully navigate the best routes in the dense undergrowth, and so we moved quietly, inspecting the environment as we went. On this trail, Gambou pointed out many edible plants as we moved. There was the Koko leaves that grew along the edge of the stream we followed, and made for an excellent side dish when cut up and boiled or sautéed. There were also bright yellow nuts that grew on thin, flowering vines. When the shell was cracked, small black kernels were found inside, and tasted very much like roasted corn nuts. In these highland forests, we also found wild coffee trees, whose bright red-ripe cherries we greedily ate as we moved.

Gambou was skilled at calling in forest duikers with his nasally call. While we marked up the trail, I urged Gambou to call for duikers whenever we came upon a suitable spot. We had great luck calling in the common blue duikers- a rabbit-sized antelope- in this particular patch of forest. Every hour or so he would call in a new antelope. So consistent was his success in calling, that I took the opportunity to begin photographing the animals.

By the second day of calling, I was beginning to practice calling for myself. Of course, I had to endure the many embarrassing moments when Gambou would burst into laughter at my failed attempts. Sometimes, my calls were so bad, we would hear distant duikers in the forest tearing away in retreat. Eventually, I somehow found the right sound, and by some miracle, called in my first duiker.

As the tiny charcoal colored antelope scurried through the undergrowth towards us, wagging its tail like a happy little puppy, Gambou's eyes lit up like a proud father. "You are a real African now," he said chuckling after the animal had departed. "I have never seen a *munju* call a duiker before."

On the third day, while the men were wrapping up with their work on the trail, Gambou and I took the opportunity to hunt on the soft forest floor that had recently been wetted by a heavy rain during the night. This act of nature would give us unbelievably silent conditions for which to sneak around the forest in.

At one point, in a section of trail that we cleared, Gabmou and I both stopped in unison- as if some unspoken sixth-sense implored us in the same moment. Carefully edging along a large fallen log, Gambou stopped and smiled as wide as a child. Coming up to his rear, I peered down in a crook of the fallen tree, and found a blue duiker antelope curled up in a ball, fast asleep. Gambou covered his mouth, on the verge of bursting into laughter at the spectacle. Duiker are perhaps the most skittish of all animals in their forest sanctuary, and getting within a hundred yards of one without it hearing us would be an accomplishment, let alone a few feet. We watched the tiny creature as it peacefully slept, its ribs rising and falling with each breath, interrupted by the occasional twitch of its nose or limbs. Finally, a small forest bird blew our cover with a shrill alarm call, sending the duiker running wildly in escape.

For the next 5 years, I would go on to collect many more such memories with my friend Gambou. We would work together professionally on hunting safaris with wealthy clients, and then less formally on road cutting expeditions deep in the bush. Always, we held the utmost respect for one another, and our close friendship never once got in the way of us performing our duties for the good of the company.

With Gambou, my hunting team was also joined by a young man named Allen, and an older guy named Charles. Allen was the youngest of the group but by far the most impressively built, with chiseled shoulders and chest that would make any steroid user in the West envious of. Charles was a thin, wiry man with a permanent mischievous twinkle fixed in his eyes. As a unit, the four of us made for an elite hunting team. I would often joke that Gambou had the gifted nose for smelling game, Allen the sensitive ears for hearing game, and Charles the sharp eyesight for spotting game; and this absolutely described their skills perfectly.

Our brotherhood was not so unlike that of military men sharing combat. With these three men I endured some of the most physically and mentally trying events of my life. We cut hundreds of miles of new 4x4 tracts deep in unchartered African bush, often getting caught in lighting storms, flash floods, swarming bee attacks, and innumerable close calls with dangerous wildlife.

Once, while spitting up to track a wounded bushbuck, I heard Gambou and Allen screaming just out of sight in a dry river bed to my right. Running around a bend in the forest, I found Gambou struggling to rack a round in the rifle he carried as the bushbuck charged at him furiously, horns down. A tangle of vines had caught the animal's chest, preventing it from stabbing Gambou. Just then, Allen leaped down from the steep bank, swinging down his machete, severing the antelopes spine and killing it.

We would also inevitably each fall under various illnesses that plagued that part of the world, and in turn, each played caregiver for one another. In fact, it was these men who helped aid me when I fell ill with dysentery, even helping me with the unspeakable act of defecation when I could no longer hold myself up.

These trials we shared together set us apart from other hunting teams in the company. My work in the bush cutting new roads was voluntary and not something I got paid for; most other guides in the company opted out of such work, and decided to spend their down-time in camp. This meant their trackers spent most of their time working away in the bush. Not surprisingly, the bonds I built with my trackers were stronger than others.

I did my best to further solidify this trust by sharing some of my disproportionately larger safari tip money with them. When the other guides heard about this, some criticized my actions as naive; citing that the Africans would take advantage of this kindness. I ignored them, and in turn, was rewarded with hard work and loyalty from my men that was not shared throughout the company. When other guides had to constantly push their trackers to produce success- it was my trackers who often pushed me to success.

The loyalty these African men had for me is difficult to describe in words. In 2012, when an armed Sudanese cow herder screamed and threatened me with his AK-47 while we were on a hunt- my trackers made sure not to let the incident slide. The encounter left a dark impression on me, and it took a long time for the anxiety of the event to wear off. My trackers saw how much it affected me.

Months later, when I was back in America awaiting the start of the next season, Gambou and Allen were sitting outside of their houses along Bakouma's main road, when a group of Sudanese cow herders- including the young man who had pointed his weapon at me- emerged to try and buy supplies. Gambou and Allen quickly located my third tracker, Charles, and the three of them promptly went to the local military outpost, where they told the soldiers about the incident in which my life was threatened by the Sudanese man. My trackers even motivated the soldiers to administer justice with some cash. Needless to say, the men were delighted when the soldiers quickly apprehended the perpetrator and proceeded to tie him up and beat him senseless; but not before making sure he understood the errors of his ways.

"We told him not to fuck with our *patron* ever again," Gambou laughed as he excitedly shared the story with me the next season.

I was more than a little horrified to learn that a man had been violently beaten at my expense. However, I would be lying if I said this gesture of loyalty wasn't touching to me- albeit in some grim way. In this lawless place, such actions held subliminal significance that would be difficult to explain in the Western world.

Even as I write this, the term "tracker" doesn't seem fitting for the men whose mentorship allowed for me to find success as a Professional Hunter. Without these local bushmen, who have always existed in the shadows alongside the white protagonists in the annals of sporting literature, there would truly never be sporting literature to even write about. And if there's a message I would like to impart on any would-be hunter hoping to travel to Africa, its this: Do not take for granted those surly, able men in the background, silently facilitating your experience in that harsh landscape. Though they might look poor and wear rags for clothing, they hold a wealth of knowledge worthy of humbly learning.

Chapter 18: Stories in the Soil

I often feel the need to clear something up regarding hunting in Central Africa: unlike other places in Africa, nowhere here can you expect to drive up on unwitting animals standing docilly in the open and shoot them. First, game densities here are far lower than the more iconic places in Africa, where scenes of migrating animals on endless plains come to mind. Secondly, the bush is so thick here, it is often impossible to spot game even if they were standing right in front of you. For savanna species like Giant eland and buffalo, this means the hunter is forced to pursue their prey by only one means available: setting off on foot and tracking them.

There are no instructional manuals to teach a person how to track. It is something learned intuitively, over many hours spent following animals. This is why a Westerner will never come close to acquiring the skills that the Africans who were born and raised in the bush possess. However, with attention and effort, even a traveling sportsman can become proficient enough to acquire a more than rudimentary tracking ability.

When you first fall in line behind the trackers as they pursue a herd of buffalo or eland, it feels like you are aimlessly walking through indefinable wilderness. But follow their eyes to the marks on the ground, and you will realize the animals have written a story in the soil, and the trackers are reading that story.

Each story left in the soil might contain similar elements, even if they lead to a different conclusion. For example, the biggest tracks, whose edges are sharply defined even in hard, rocky ground- belong to the herd bull. They move straight, purposefully. So too do the worn edges of a medium sized track- most likely the herd matriarch. They too move with purpose and do not stray from the course. The more common tracks of the subadults wander slightly as they feed whenever they can. The tiniest tracks, belonging to the calves, move in a finicky nature- as do all children of every species.

The story in the soil might tell of thirst, as the passing of 30 animals or more are reduced to tiny scuff marks on rocky ground, pulled by an invisible string to a tiny pool of stagnant water on an otherwise barren plateau. How they arrive exactly to this small puddle after crossing dozens of miles feels like a miracle in itself. The moods of the animals are defined in the soil too. Wandering tracks spread in all directions suggest the herd's desire to stop and feed, and the reader of the track best be prepared to soon meet the animals. When the smallest tracks stubbornly begin heading straight to cover, pulling the larger tracks with them, the reader can be sure the needs of the tiny ones will implore the herd to lay in rest in the nearest patch of shade.

In time, subtle nuances can be seen in the story- tiny footnotes barely noticed at first. Little bits of saliva-covered leaves left on the ground after falling out of greedy eland lips. Dark patches of ground indicating a dribble of urine. Even discarded semen from a breeding bull buffalo who missed his mark. An angry Puff adder left hissing among the torn up ground where a group of heavy animals disturbed his peace. All of these little details add to the story.

Although there might be consistent patterns to the soil's story, no two tales read the same, as I learned during my first eland safari.

My American hunter was in his 60s, and although he was a seasoned African hunter, he was a hopelessly bad shot. The year before, a French PH had guided him in our concession, and after missing a big bull eland early in the hunt, he ended up mistakenly shooting a juvenile near the end of his safari. Worst of all, it had taken five shots to kill the poor animal, ranging from a gut shot, thigh shot, and eventually, into the vitals. He was returning to hunt with me on a discounted price, to make good on the errors he had made his previous safari. Erik was eager to get the man his eland and be done with it, and he did not mince his words when he demanded my success. The pressure loomed over me the entire safari.

Finding fresh eland sign to follow was always half the battle, as the animals migrated to and fro like caribou across the arctic tundra. Where hundreds might be feeding on a plateau one day, might suddenly vanish for a hundred miles in all directions the next day. Luckily, in a rocky woodland at the heart of the Ngoy hunting area, we encountered multiple herds of eland and were able to track them nearly every day.

It was during this two-week safari that I truly appreciated how difficult it was to hunt Lord Derby's eland. Almost every day we would follow fresh tracks crossing a road in the morning, and end up catching the animals in the afternoon. The problem was, every time we caught up to the animals close enough to see them, we only had a matter of seconds before one of them spotted us, and they would flee into the wind. This became a disappointing pattern that left me with lingering PTSD; it got to the point that whenever my tracker would hiss and point out the animals hiding in a thicket, it was not excitement I felt, but dread. I knew it was only a matter of time before the animals would see or smell us, and the hunt would be over.

So difficult are Lord Derby's eland to hunt, that even after years of bowhunting public land in the American West and successfully stalking and killing a number of high-country mule deer and bull elk in their day beds- it is still my opinion that none of these hunts compare in difficulty to the Lord Derby's eland.

As a rookie, one of my mistakes was that I was too hesitant and careful that first safari. Instead of taking advantage of those early seconds and trying to quickly get in a position to shoot a bull when the herd milled about confused- I would try to stalk even closer with painstaking care. This almost never worked, as the watchful eyes of an old cow would inevitably spot us first.

One day, however, my strategy almost worked- perhaps just by dumb luck. When a herd was located on a small hill covered in thick trees, I instructed the trackers to stay back as the client and I belly crawled for a 100 yards. Soon, we got behind a termite mound in position to shoot a massive bull bedded just in front of us. When the wind changed, as it was bound to do, the herd stood up about to take flight. But to our luck, the big bull stood broadside to us with nothing blocking the bullet's path. The hunt was in the bag, and even a child could not have missed that shot.

I still see the image of that bull in my mind, standing there impossibly big with his swollen black neck and flapping throat dewlap.

The rifle boomed, but the bull did not move. It boomed again and again- finally sending the confused bull running straight toward us. The man missed again, this time at a distance of 40 yards. Finally, the animals spotted us and turned the other direction. Soon, only a dust cloud indicated their passing.

I was stunned to the point of speechlessness. The client's face was white like a ghost. My trackers were beyond irritated, cursing the man in Sango under their breaths. The poor fellow had such bad buck fever that even a full ten minutes later, his arms were still shaking uncontrollably. I never spoke about the incident to the man. There was no need to. The only thing left to do was to put our heads down and get back to work, and hope, against all odds, we could have another opportunity like that.

As the days ticked by, the eland opportunities evaporated, and a panic began to set in. It was beginning to feel like the second half of the safari was going to be a dud. Alas, we got our lucky break on the second to last day of the safari, when I decided to change things up and hunt the Kocho and Chinko plateaus (not far from where tracker Mohomet had first taught me how to hunt eland when we slept on the animals' tracks during my apprenticeship).

When tracking eland nonstop for two weeks, the eyes get lulled into complacency when staring at the same sign on the ground. But it is this complacency that sabotages the success of the hunt. No matter how tired, thirsty, or burnt-out one might feel- a skilled hunter must force themselves to remain focused- to read each sentence of the story unfolding in the dirt, regardless of the similarities. It was reading this sign that we saw something we had never seen before.

Arriving to a large spot of torn up ground on a flat plateau, we were shocked to find chunks of black eland neck hair and spots of blood. After some investigation, it became clear that two big bulls in the herd had been fighting. Perhaps they were vying for a position to breed a prized female in heat.

Eland bulls often travel together with breeding herds, but fights apparently rarely occur. In fact, when I told this story to experienced hunters in the past, they simply thought I misread the sign. Recently, my friend PH Thierry Labat captured photos of Lord Derby's eland bulls fighting in Cameroon, a revelation that has vindicated my claim.

Excited by this rare event, we continued following the sign. Soon after we arrived to an open plain stretching for miles in all directions. I was confused, because the eland track had been so fresh, the animals could not have been more than a few hundred yards in front of us; but the plain remained empty. A small thicket full of wild coffee trees lay in front of us, and I decided to post up there to assess the situation.

As we approached from an angle, our perspective of the patch of grassland just beyond the thicket suddenly changed, and there, frozen like statues, stood approximately 40 eland bunched up together, looking at us wide-eyed.

Two big bulls stood facing each other in front of the herd- apparently the ones which had been fighting. As the cows and young behind these animals turned to run, the two bulls stayed frozen, leaving a clear shot. As calmly as I could, I instructed the hunter to shoot the larger of the two. Blessedly, he made the shot count, and we were soon standing over the first Giant eland bull of my career.

Though it was not my personal trophy, it is difficult to describe the overwhelming feeling of contentment and pride I felt in that moment as I graced my hands over that special animal. I felt pride for myself, for my hunting team, and even for the nervous old hunter- who had overcome his debilitating buck fever long enough to shoot straight.

There is a photo of my standing behind this eland, holding its horns up with both hands and leaning over it in reverence. To this day, this is one of my most prized hunting photos. And when I see it- I am reminded of the entire story of that hunt, etched out in the dry African soil.

Although I loved the challenge of hunting eland, they were almost too difficult to the point of not being enjoyable. On the trail of buffalo, in contrast, I enjoyed every minute of the pursuit. This is not to say tracking buffalo were easy; on the contrary, they were often exceptionally difficult to hunt. However, success still felt attainable- unlike many of the eland hunts. There was, of course, the added aspect of danger tied to buffalo hunts that added to their appeal.

My first buffalo hunt took place with a wily old German man in his late 60s, and his even more wily and older companion, who could have been in his early 80s. This companion turned out to be a humble legend in himself. It was revealed to me in the course of the hunt that this man had hunted all over Africa in the 1960s and into the early 2000s. He had even hunted in the northern Central African Republic in the 60s, before the poaching had decimated much of the megafauna. He told us about a black and white photo in his trophy room back in Germany, where he is standing behind a Lord Derby's eland with his French Professional Hunter, and in the foreground, stands a big, irritated Black rhinoceros. The animal had been laying in a nearby thicket when the man shot the eland, and only emerged after the commotion the men made when they approached the fallen antelope.

With these men, I hoped to successfully track down and shoot a big buffalo bull that had eluded numerous guides at a nearby lake it was often seen at. Anton had warned me that the hunt was futile- that he had long since given up trying to track the red buffalo at the lake. But I didn't believe him. I would have to learn the hard way myself.

That first morning, we arrived at the lake early, and soon enough- spotted the notorious buffalo and his herd of cows and young. Immediately, we began tracking them. Soon, they took us on a huge loop of the area, over steep hills, down in swampy ravines, and finally, back at the lake's edge- before starting the loop all over again.

Though the Africans were superior trackers, their skills at stalking animals were not always practical for the modern sport hunter. Since they grew up in the bush hunting with homemade shotguns, the goal for the African hunter is to sneak as closely as possible to the nearest animal, regardless of sex, age, or trophy size. I learned this the hard way on this buffalo hunt.

Whenever we found the buffalo herd bedded in a thicket, the trackers would push me frantically to get closer to the animals, but without strategizing how to reach the bull. Soon, my German hunters and I would be crawling on our hands and knees into the thick buffalo lairs. This brought us frighteningly close to the animals on three different occasions. The only problem was, we would find ourselves surrounded by bedded buffalo, with no bull in sight. Inevitably, we could only stay crouched inside the bedding area for so long before the wind would change, and the animals would flee.

The last time this happened, we exited the thicket and stood there, contemplating our next move. The wind had picked up and was swirling all around. As is usually the case with swirling wind, the buffalo could not pinpoint our exact location, and began running wildly in all directions. Suddenly, the confused animals did a 180 degree turn, and came stampeding towards us, unseen behind a wall of dense bush. We heard the thundering approach, but we could not tell exactly where the animals would emerge.

I instructed the men to get ready. I told the younger of the two hunters to rest his rifle on the shooting sticks and wait for my command. I knew the animals would stop when they saw us, perhaps giving us just enough time to locate the bull and shoot.

Just as I predicted, the bush tore open in front of us, and the streaming wall of buffalo suddenly stopped, 30 yards away. But before I could locate the bull, there was a barrage of booming shots to my right, and my world suddenly went deaf. Cursing, I turned and found my frightened client shooting wildly into the herd. This sent the animals thundering away once again.

I could not contain my range and began screaming at the man, asking him what in the hell he was doing.

"I thought they were going to attack us," he said, almost on the verge of tears.

I decided the man was sufficiently chastised, and didn't bother him about it again. We followed the buffalo for the rest of the day, carefully looking for any sign of a wounded animal the hunter might have shot. Alas, we found nothing, and I concluded the man had missed the animals altogether- something shocking in itself, since he fired at them from a distance of about 30 yards.

We wasted an entire week fruitlessly hunting the lake buffalo, before finally retiring from the endeavor, just as Anton had predicted we would. Now, the safari was nearing its conclusion, and the pressure to succeed weighed heavy on my rookie mind once again.

On the very last day of the hunt, we tried our best to remain optimistic, but the prospects of success were looking dim. We set off in the morning following a fresh rain, and soon located the tracks of a herd of buffalo that had crossed the road just hours before. If tracking an animal is like reading nature's storybook, on this day, the story read as easily as a children's book. Even a novice could have followed the tracks as they sunk deeply into the rain-muddied ground. It was a blessing we had earned from all the previous days of hard work that had led us to that point.

We caught the herd feeding on a patch of bright new grass that looked like it could have grown on a luxury golf course. The animals were feeding placidly between two forest edges, giving us ample cover to stalk closer. There was a nervous pit in my stomach, because everything was falling into place too perfectly, and I expected it to collapse at any moment. We were even able to crawl behind a massive termite mound, and watched as the herd bull separated from the cows and began to feed closer to us. The man could have shot the bull with my open sighted rifle, it was so close.

Three shots anchored the bull. As he lay there, eyes glazing over, he let out the eerie death bellow the animals are famous for. It was only the second time I had heard the noise, and I had to turn away from the clients as tears welled in my eyes.

The story left in the soil that day wasn't over.

After quartering the buffalo, we set off to fetch the truck. As we flanked the edge of the forest, we came to a patch of long grass that looked as if it had just been matted down. Almost anyone else would have walked past the spot without noticing it, but my trackers could read something that I had missed. Another story had played out here just hours before our arrival, and the men let me follow the clues for myself, before they painted the picture for me.

Thin splashes of blood dripped from the tips of the rain-covered grass, almost unnoticeable at first. Leaning in closer, I found tufts of hair and flesh scattered about. Then, I began to notice chunks of grass pulled from the roots, with deep claw marks creating numerous ruts in the ground. Finally, I arrived to the last clue- a pile of discarded aardvark claws with flesh still attached. I looked up, and my trackers smiled, knowing I had finally read the story that had taken them only seconds to comprehend.

A massive leopard had confronted a large aardvark outside of its den earlier that morning and a vicious battle ensued. From the chunks of flesh with leopard hair attached, it appeared the aardvark had got some serious licks in on the cat. The animals thrashed around over a large area. Finally, after an undoubtedly exhausting battle, the leopard managed to kill the aardvark. But the cat had only a brief moment to feed on its prize, before it was forced to limp off into the forest when the hyenas arrived to forcefully take over the rest of the kill.

    I explained the scene to the two old hunters, and they marveled at the sight, putting their hands in the earth and feeling the elements of the story for themselves. In that moment, I realized so much has been lost to the modern hunter. We put all of the emphasis on the equipment and the kill of the hunt- we miss the main elements of the stories themselves. Central Africa might not have its plains full of migrating animals. It might be a hot, thick, insect-infested wasteland. Sportsman might have to hunt ten-times as hard here for only a fraction of the trophies. But few places left in the world offer the hunter a chance to participate in nature's story like they do here.

    Every day, everywhere, in wild places across the world- beautiful, wonderous, savage stories are waiting to be read.

Closing: The Elephant in the Room

As I sit back, reflecting on my time in the bush now more than a decade removed- those five years felt like a lifetime, but I know they were short compared to the careers of many PHs. It gave me enough time to dip my feet in and taste the experience of being a Professional Hunter, but short enough that I humbly accept there was still much more to be learned.

In general, I was a gifted hunter, but my skills were generalized; I was a jack-of-all-trades, but a master of none. I think I was an excellent eland hunter, for example, but my knowledge of leopard and big buffalo needed more improving. The other thing I realized, was that in order to be a good PH, one must possess good people skills, and not just hunting skills. And in this regard, I was not gifted. My clients were successful at taking the animals they wanted, but I was often harsh and pushed them. I also alienated myself because I kept a strict ethical standard of hunting that was unrealistic to many of them. Ultimately, I decided being a PH was not a career I wanted to continue for the rest of my life.

The truth is, simply becoming a licensed PH was a childhood dream of mine, and to accomplish that dream at such a young age is a blessing not many people have the opportunity to be able to achieve.

That said, one of the biggest rewards of being able to accomplish this goal, was to work with so many legendary Professional Hunters. In compiling these stories in this book, I am in no way putting myself on their same level. I was a rookie, and with that position, I am obligated to thank each of them for being gracious colleagues and teaching me skills to help me become a better outdoorsman. This thank you extends to Mike Fell, Thierry Labat, Pete Wood, Dan Moore, Francois Guillet, Christophe Moreo, Philippe Cléro, Erik Mararv, Anton Lundkvisk and last but not least, my little brother turned mentor- Erik Nyman. And beyond these men, I need to pay brief homage to other legendary PHs who came before me and paved the way in this particular region of Africa. PHs like Rudy Lubin, Alain Lefol, Jacques Lemaux, Jean and Matthieu Laboureur- to give a nod to just a few.

Like most men who enter this profession, I found myself disillusioned by the steady destruction of wildlife I witnessed on the African continent at the hands of poaching and landscape degradation. It is a complex issue that has been debated and analyzed to death by many brilliant minds, and it's not something I can solve in a short closing paragraph. In the end, human nature is a powerful force, and both money and poverty can be overwhelming catalysts of destruction if they are not managed properly.

The elephant in the room in my story, is the fact that I have very little material for which to write about the one animal that was, at one point in history, synonymous with the very place I write about: the African elephant.

There was a time in the not-so-distant past, in my father's generation- that the eastern two-thirds of the Central African Republic, with the Chinko basin at the center, was perhaps the most promising elephant population in Sub-Sahara Africa. In his book, *African Silences*, famous naturalist Peter Matthiessen suggests there were perhaps 100,000 elephants here before 1970. Stories of big tuskers seemingly hiding behind every bush are legendary. In his excellent book, *On Target:*

History and Hunting in Central Africa, PH Christian Le Noel includes many vintage photos and stories of the elephants taken in this region pre-1970. The photographs of the lengths of some of the ivory defy the imagination.

…. Today, we are lucky if only 200 elephants survive in an area the size of my home state of Kansas.

I do not know if it was simply a lucky fluke, but in 2011, while driving back to the Kocho Airstrip from the Ngoy camp, a bull elephant slowly crossed the road in front of my Land Cruiser at less than 100 yards. Myself and the two local Africans accompanying me stared in disbelief at the tusks of the elephant, which were nearly touching the ground. It was only the eighth elephant I had ever seen in the Chinko basin. Within two days, a line of smoke aggressively spreading hundreds of miles from the north finally reached our area, signaling the arrival of a large caravan of Janjaweed elephant hunters from Sudan with their donkeys. They were tracking this very bull and his small herd.

Talking to the old timers who worked this area in the 70s and 80s is depressing. When a grizzled old PH Fred Duckworth came to visit our camp in the Chinko basin one season, he couldn't help but grumble about how drastically the landscape had changed since he was last there- when the elephants roamed unmolested. And I don't blame him; had I seen the place back then, perhaps I would have the same bleak outlook on the area's future.

Alas, one silver-lining to being born late and missing this wildlife boon, is the fact that my young optimism still exists: in the absence of the large herds of elephant, the region still feels like a paradise worth protecting- with its herds of roaming eland and bongo, lion and leopard. And this optimism is needed if each proceeding generation is to draw a line in the sand and protect what remaining paradise is left.

Most people's view of the mechanisms of conservation are ambiguous: we are content with the idea that a lot of money thrown into a problem will help to alleviate it. But in African conservation, money is simply a tool for a larger, more complex process. And in that process, land preservation is perhaps the most important piece of the puzzle.

Money keeps hunting outfitters in large areas of land that would otherwise be destroyed by cattle herders and meat poachers; this is undeniable when looking at the history of Sub-Saharan land development. The significance of this fact can be demonstrated when considering the African lion: in countries where lion hunting is still legal, lion habitat makes up nearly one-third of all land occupied by lions (the majority existing in national parks, with some existing in communal lands). If sport hunting were to be outlawed, the entire population of lions on the continent would likely drop by one-third.

Still, the presence of hunting outfitters on the land can only hold so much power in the face of such overwhelming exploitation by desperate people.

From our perspective at CAWA safaris, we witnessed firsthand how hunting can be a tool for conservation and wild land preservation. Our presence alone there prevented much wildlife destruction for a few years. But even our impact became overwhelmed by the sheer scale of the destruction when cattle-herding refugees from Chad and Sudan migrated to the area and decimated the wildlife. By then, even the $200,000 contribution our biggest client made each season, and the dozens of other clients paying upwards of $100,000- still wasn't enough to save the land. Ultimately, in desperation of losing our beloved wilderness and its unique wildlife, we had to turn to *African Parks*- a non-hunting conservation entity- to save the area with the extensive resources they had that we did not. Today, *African Parks* is doing a masterful job managing the Chinko Reserve- the very hunting concessions we formerly operated in.

As a hunter, I feel obligated to speak to the hunting community in regard to conservation. I would be beating a dead horse if I continued to comment on the counterproductive nature of anti-hunting groups, whose misguided efforts to stop regulated sport hunting have only further harmed wildlife on the continent. Still, I also cannot deny the fact that as a hunting outfitter, we could not protect our hunting unit in the Central African Republic by ourselves, and we needed to collaborate with a non-hunting entity in order to save it. This is why, as a hunter, I plead with hunting groups to keep an open-mind and consider collaboration beyond our own industry.

We as hunters know that it is not the well-regulated and sustainable sport hunting industry that is destroying wildlife in Africa, but the desperation of poor meat hunters and land-hungry pastoralists. In the face of such overwhelming odds, I think its naïve to think hunting dollars alone are enough to save the wildlife on the continent- and I'm getting tired of so many powerful hunting clubs clinging to this delusion. We cannot continue to have groups of individual entities with their own individual interests trying to protect the wildlife on the continent and hope to achieve large-scale success. Collaboration across various governmental and private sectors seems an undeniable next step in preserving African wildlife for future generations.

I still find it interesting that in my handful of years working as a PH, many of the wealthy hunters who considered themselves "conservationists," would often lament about how there were not enough tigers left in the world for them to hunt, instead of lamenting on the creature's precarious place at the edge of extinction itself. I wonder then, when the poaching reaches such an extreme state that the population of African lion and elephant dips so low that even regulated hunting is outlawed- will these hunter "conservationists" step in with their resources and save the wildlife? Or are they only willing to save that which they can kill? These are not questions I claim to have the answers for. But in looking at the long-term future of both sport hunting and conservation in Africa- I think there are many more uncomfortable questions to be had.

Acknowledgments

Thanks to both my parents for fostering in me a love for the outdoors. Thanks to Luis Prendes for being the first person to teach me how to hunt and fish. Thanks to Erik Mararv and the rest of the Mararv family- as well as Emelie Nestor- for allowing me the opportunity to follow my dreams in Africa. Thanks to Peter Flack for helping me get my foot in the door in my writing career. Thanks to all the Professional Hunters who guided me along in my journey, who I previously mentioned in closing. Thanks to Thaddeus Eshelman for supporting my work and giving me the time to complete the first drafts of my books. And lastly, thank you to my children for continuing to inspire my adventures outdoors, and helping me prioritize the important things in life.

Chapter 1: A version of this story first appeared in *Sports Afield* (March/April 2018)

Chapter 4: A version of this story first appeared in *Sports Afield* (January/February 2016)

Chapter 6: A version of this story first appeared in Peter Flack's *Hunting the Spiral Horns: Bushbuck* (2014)

Chapter 11: A version of this story first appeared in *Sporting Classics* (March/April 2016)

Chapter 14: A version of this story first appeared in *Magnum* (SA) (April 2016)

Chapter 16: A version of this story first appeared in *Magnum* (SA) (Spring 2013)

Adam Parkison is a former Professional Hunter in Africa who now works as a freelance writer and photographer covering wild places. His work has appeared in *Sidetracked, Backcountry Journal, Sports Afield, Sporting Classics, Bow and Arrow*, and more. Adam has a bachelor's degree in journalism and media communication from Colorado State University. He currently lives in Colorado with his two children.

www.ingramcontent.com/pod-product-compliance
Lightning Source LLC
Chambersburg PA
CBHW060951050426
42337CB00054B/3897